CUPID IS
STUPID!

How to
Fall in
Love
Without
Falling
on Your
Face

William L. Coleman

INTERVARSITY PRESS
DOWNERS GROVE, ILLINOIS 60515

All rights reserved. No part of this book may be reproduced in any form without written permission from InterVarsity Press, P.O. Box 1400, Downers Grove, Illinois 60515.

InterVarsity Press is the book-publishing division of InterVarsity Christian Fellowship, a student movement active on campus at hundreds of universities, colleges and schools of nursing in the United States of America, and a member movement of the International Fellowship of Evangelical Students. For information about local and regional activities, write Public Relations Dept., InterVarsity Christian Fellowship, 6400 Schroeder Rd., P.O. Box 7895, Madison, WI 53707-7895.

All Scripture quotations, unless otherwise indicated, are from the Holy Bible, New International Version. Copyright © 1973, 1978, International Bible Society. Used by permission of Zondervan Bible Publishers.

Cover illustration: Tim Nyberg

ISBN 0-8308-1335-7

Printed in the United States of America ∞

Library of Congress Cataloging-in-Publication Data has been requested.

15	*14*	*13*	*12*	*11*	*10*	*9*	*8*	*7*	*6*	*5*	*4*	*3*	*2*	*1*
03	*02*	*01*	*00*	*99*	*98*	*97*	*96*	*95*	*94*	*93*	*92*	*91*		

*To Mary Coleman
and June Coleman:*

*Thanks for teaching me
about love . . .
and thanks for helping
with this book.*

Who
Reads
This?

*B*ecause you picked up this book, I assume you must have
some great qualities. I suppose the reader is deeply into hope and dreams
and heartfelt emotions. The reader wants to take risks, stick his neck out
and try one of the most fantastic experiences any human can share.

You must have curiosity and be willing to take a close look at intimacy,
sharing and openness. You want to explore how you feel, how you ought
to feel and maybe how you could feel if only you allowed yourself the
freedom. You wonder how two people become united, how they split a
leftover pizza slice and how they choose a movie.

The reader must also be a believer. Skeptics, pessimists and grouches
would have trouble reading about love. They aren't sure that love exists
or is worth pursuing. Whoever travels through these pages must have

faith that love could rise up and embrace two people . . . that love could transform two independent, unique souls into one caring, giving, couple.

You sound like an intriguing person. Until we're able to meet in a more personal setting, I am glad that a subject as enriching as love could bring us together.

1
What Is Couple Love?

*W*e are going to discuss how people love each other. Where does love come from? How do we recognize it? How can we cause it to grow? How can we protect love? And what about the good feelings that go along with it?

Ask yourself these questions:

■ Have you ever been so glad to see someone that you began to salivate?

■ Have you ever wanted to be near a person so strongly that you have felt your heart ache?

■ Have you caught yourself staring out the window daydreaming about someone with whom you recently spent time?

■ Have you ever written a person's name over and over on a piece of paper or on the cover of a notebook?

If you have had experiences similar to these, or if you'd like to, you might find this book extremely helpful. Those are the kinds of questions that will be raised and dealt with.

The issue here is people love. We won't handle the tricky problems of why we love chocolate, automobiles or bird soup. We narrow the field to people, particularly couples. If loving is worthwhile (and it certainly is), then love is something we should learn about.

What Is Couple Love?

There is a phrase which applies perfectly here. The old saying goes, "I may not know what it is, but I can recognize it when I see it."

Love doesn't have a tidy definition. Love isn't necessarily a certain size or color, and love doesn't live in a particular habitat. But when we see love in action, we know what's going on.

Don't stumble over the definition. Don't waste time asking if love is metaphysical, existential or egocentric. Love is best understood by what it does and does not do.

Thousands of years ago a wise person threw up his hands and said in effect, "Who can understand the love a man has for a woman?" (Prov 30:19). Why do his bushy eyebrows turn you on, and those same eyebrows frighten someone else? Why do you adore her witty remarks, and a friend thinks she's boring? That's a mystery.

Let's leave it a mystery. We have little choice anyway.

But love is real. We can't see wind, but it exists. Faith has no form, but we see its effects. Trust can't be bought in handy packets at the store. Our lives are filled with experiences that we can never hold, see, smell or taste.

Ask a twenty-year-old wife whose husband is away for six months in the Navy. Ask if love is real. Ask her if love hurts. Does love hope, does it long, does love plan, does it anticipate? Don't ask her to define it. Merely ask what love does.

A Powerful Hold

The love we have for another person becomes one of the most compelling forces in the world. And we don't just mean our sex drive. Beyond that we have an overwhelming desire to be with the person we love. We want his presence, his personality, his brightness, his reassurance, his companionship.

Caught in the avalanche of love, people have sacrificed their scholarships, their careers, their friends, their hobbies and their families to be near the person of their dreams. The Song of Songs says it accurately: "For love is as strong as death" (8:6).

Love reportedly caused Nebuchadnezzar to build the famous "Hanging Gardens of Babylon." He didn't want his charming bride to become homesick for the mountains of her homeland.

More recently a man in South Carolina hired a helicopter to drop 2,500 carnations and 10,000 love letters on the lawn of his former girlfriend. She failed to appreciate his display of affection, and the would-be Romeo was charged with littering.

Not everyone loses his mind to this degree. Many of us manage to fulfill our other responsibilities with reasonable calm. But many lovers are driven somewhat crazy by this strong emotion.

Once the spark catches flame, love can shortly turn into a raging fire. Those fires burn deeply and are not usually put out easily. Someone who had experience with such love wrote: "Many waters cannot quench love; rivers cannot wash it away" (Song 8:7).

Love is a mystery, and love is terribly strong. Love even has some of the markings of madness. Despite its complexity, love is a force that few of us would care to miss. We want to sit by the flame, feel its warmth, enjoy love's beauty.

This Cupid Business

Because love often is elusive, powerful and bewildering, because love can both bless and curse, because love isn't tangible, we like to playfully blame it all on Cupid. Not that we actually believe in a genuine, pudgy, cherublike creature with a bow and arrow; but frequently we want to assign the responsibility for love to realms beyond our control. We have a Cupid mentality.

Cupid comes to us from a couple of sources. To the Greeks he was Eros, and to the Romans he was Amor, or Cupid. Eventually he evolved into a matchmaker who had the power to bring couples together. From early on he possessed both a happy and a cruel nature.

In physical form Cupid was an athletic, handsome character. By the middle 300s B.C. he was demoted to the chubby, naked creature we know today. Equipped with wings, Cupid's job is to fly about with a bow and arrows looking for people to shoot. Anyone who is pierced with such an arrow falls deliriously in love.

It's all fun and games except for an underlying problem. Too many of us want to wash our hands of the responsibility for love.

We want to say love isn't my fault.

I have no power over who I love.

I can't help it if I fall in love.

I can't help it if I fall out of love.

Love just hasn't hit me yet.

We are tempted to give love a life of its own. As if love comes and goes, smiles and frowns, awakes or sleeps purely on its own terms. If you and I can't control love, who can then? Let's blame it on Cupid.

Cupid represents an outside force. Cupid makes judgments. Cupid is fickle and manipulative. And this is why Cupid is stupid.

We want to make Cupid a scapegoat . . . make the round-chested twit take all the blame.

But, we rightfully protest, we don't actually believe in a real Cupid. However, if we picture love as an irresistible, uncontrollable, outside force, we play with a Cupid mentality. And our love suffers from it.

Love is a mystery, but it isn't all mystery.

Love is teachable.

Love is controllable.

Love is preventable.

Love is stoppable.

Love is encourageable.

Love is reinforceable.

Love is manageable. We have a tremendous amount of influence on couple love. This is true if we are twenty years old and in love for the first time, if we are celebrating our fifteenth anniversary or if we are marrying again later in life. Love can be directed if we choose to take the steering wheel.

None of us needs to fear love, but we should show it a healthy respect. There are dangers afoot. At the same time love holds the prospect of incredible satisfaction. Couple love is good. Life offers nothing quite like it.

Understand love as best you're able. Find a person who hums your tune. Then love that one with all the energy, passion and commitment you can deliver.

2
Jumping
in
Love

I didn't actually fall in love with my wife, Pat, but I knew I could. We went to the same small college and were aware of each other for a couple of years. As I saw Pat in classrooms or in the hall, the thought entered my mind many times that she was first-class. More than once I said to myself that some lucky guy was going to get her.

Mentally I had no doubt that if I got to know Pat I could love her. Only time and space stood between us. During those years, I dated others and never dreamed she would go out with me. But, if it ever happened, I knew she would have it all.

Eventually a friend "pushed" me into asking her out. After two weeks of dating I made another calculation. I knew I wanted to marry her.

At first I wasn't dizzy in love. When I ate lunch, I didn't eat the wrappers on my sandwiches or chew my dixie cups. But after a date or two I began howling at the moon and drooling on my jacket.

There is a sense in which I "fell" in love. But I also measured the situation and chose someone who was extremely easy to love.

The best balance seems to be in the middle. Love should be half irrational. A person ought to send off alarms in your heart and cause you to stare out the window for hours. However, the other half needs to be computerized. Why does this love make sense? How will it work? What makes us compatible?

Too many loves have become wrecked because they have had one half without the other.

Any of us could "fall" in love. Some marry and are happy as chipmunks for the next fifty years. But millions of others "fall" apart and argue over support payments. The Bible puts it well: "Above all else, guard your heart, for it is the wellspring of life" (Prov 4:23).

Unfortunately, some people spend all of their time guarding themselves, and they never do let love in. That's the other extreme.

Hang gliders appear to have gained the right attitude. They check the weather, the wind currents, the landing possibilities. When they have a good grasp of the environment, they take a firm hold of their glider and jump off the mountain.

"Jumping in love" is such a better concept than "falling." Falling sounds like an accident . . . like tripping or stumbling. It's a tad klutzy. Jumping has all the thrill of total commitment, but the jumper took time to find out what was going on.

Love and Glandular Eruptions
Some people seem to fall in love every time they walk through the mall. They see a good-looking guy or a girl in great jeans, and they suffer from a love attack. It doesn't usually last much longer than their next trip to Wal-Mart.

It's too bad that a few people are fooled by the first flush of someone's appearance. That feeling is better described as the "hots," but it definitely isn't love. It's more like a Barbie-doll syndrome.

Promise yourself that you will never choose to love someone with whom you have not had at least one intelligent conversation. Second, promise yourself that you will not date anyone twice who wears clothes more than four sizes too small for her body (like a Barbie doll).

Let No One "Steal" Your Heart

Our hearts are too valuable to leave lying around for any thief to haul off. Hearts can be stolen and frequently are. When they are taken against our better judgment, we often regret the day we let them get away.

A girl from Seattle wrote to tell me about her boyfriend. She loved him to the marrow of her bones; but, unfortunately, he treated her like dirt. He was insanely jealous, obsessively possessive, verbally abusive, painfully destructive. Toni went on to explain that they had not been happy for the past year and a half, but she still loved him. What should she do?

Toni, go collect your heart. He stole it. He isn't taking good care of it. A heart is a terrible thing to waste. Get it back before it suffers too much damage.

The Song of Songs speaks of having his heart stolen. "You have stolen my heart, my sister, my bride; you have stolen my heart with one glance of your eyes, with one jewel of your necklace" (4:9).

We all understand the feeling. How romantic can life get? But smart people keep one hand on their heart until they find the person they want to totally love. Then they let their heart be stolen.

We Control Love

The pull toward love is a strong one. We see someone, talk to him, enter his space and are drawn like gravity toward him. That is the way it was meant to be. But we don't give in to every magnetic love, for there is much more involved than attraction. We have met hundreds, if not thousands, of people we are attracted to. That doesn't mean we are compelled to love each in a romantic sense.

Love does not own us. We own love. As intelligent human beings, we resist most attractions and hold out for the "one" we choose.

God gives us instructions on how to love and whom to love because he knows it is within our power to follow his instructions. We are not lemmings racing head-on and throwing ourselves off the cliff because we refused to slow down and think it over. We each have the option to love this person or that person. Smart people hand out their love with deliberate care.

"Then they can train the younger women to love their husbands and children" (Tit 2:4).

Love is a controllable, usable passion.

3
Learning to Love

*W*hy would anyone buy a book or take a class in love? Isn't love supposed to come naturally . . . like eating or rolling over? We don't teach people to reach or to grow hair. It just happens.

All of that makes sense. Love should come naturally, too, but it doesn't. There are two reasons we usually mess it up. First, we see poor examples of love. Our role models are murky and imperfect. Movie stars, soap opera leads, young adults, even parents give us a sample of love, but they have rough edges and soiled spots. Even heroes, ministers and teachers have trouble transmitting good love vibes.

But role models are only part of the problem. If we were to see perfect examples of love, we still might not be great receivers. Even when we watch great love at work, we are usually unable to understand it and copy it on our own. That's why we need help.

Becky's parents had a smooth, happy relationship. Once in a while they hit the rumble bars of life's bumpy highways, but nothing went seriously wrong. After twenty years they still enjoyed each other's company, dated now and again and dropped over to the local pizzeria for a Coke and small talk.

Much, but not all, of their behavior automatically rubbed off on Becky. She never stopped to think through what was going on with her parents, and she couldn't see what was happening behind the scenes. What did they talk about when they were alone? What had "worked out" over the years? What were the unresolved parts of their relationship?

Becky had learned a great deal by osmosis. She absorbed it by being around genuine love, but being near love still leaves a tremendous number of unanswered questions. Becky, like the rest of us, needed some first-class pointers in love.

No one has to apologize for wanting to learn about love. It does not come naturally. If we don't learn about love, we could have a shallow concept of it all our lives. That would be a tragedy.

There are several places where love is often taught in the wrong way. We will call them Schools of Failure. They teach love in such a twisted fashion that it's hard to sift out the good from the bad.

The School of Entertainment

Let's be fair about movies and television. There are many examples of caring and genuine love in both of these media. Unfortunately, they are often drowned out by sick and inadequate forms of love. Too frequently, a man who leaves his family for another woman is treated as a hero. The audience ends up pulling for the person who has opted for an adulterous situation. If entertainment is our major school for love, our value system could easily end up godless and perverted.

I watched a great many movies as I grew up. From them I believed that women liked to be treated roughly. I thought they wanted to be told what to do, that they liked to be pushed, pulled and kissed roughly. If we adopt that as a view of love, we can mess up a relationship before it gets started. Entertainment makes a lousy primary school of love.

The School of Music
A famous song claims that God made the singer a rambling man and he can't help it. Whenever he gets the urge, the singer has to leave his family and wander for months or years. Somehow God is supposed to have given him itchy feet and he has to go out and scratch them on the highways of life—or words to that effect.

Secular music gives us some beautiful and helpful love songs, but as a school, it is spotty at best. If we listen to the words, and not everyone does, we have to think it through. Some of what is called love is no more than the impulsive hots. It isn't true love, and it will not last over the long haul. But music becomes a powerful school of a mixed view of love.

The School of Mistakes
We don't learn much about love by watching others make mistakes. When we hear of other teenagers trying to find love in the back seat of a Chevy, we don't learn much about love. If we try to copy them, we learn even less.

Young people know a tremendous amount about love. We certainly can learn by sharing with others. But we don't learn well by watching other people love poorly. Sometimes we hear how others act out their love, and we are confused as to whether that was good, bad or a combination of good and bad.

While teaching in a reform school, I was asked by a teenage inmate if I had a girlfriend, and I told him that I did. Immediately he wanted to know, in front of the class, if I had ever had sex with her. I wasn't ready for that question. Totally flustered, I told him that I hadn't, to which he added, "Then why do you have her?"

He learned his system of love from his surroundings and peers. Why anyone would hold back on sex was a new concept.

There are many other "schools" that do not teach love well. They are undependable in their values, knowledge and experience. They talk about "love" but succeed only in muddying up the subject.

If there are schools which do a poor and destructive job, where do we learn what love should really be like? Let's start off with a few suggestions.

Read a few good books that help you "think it through." Some are written well, are upbeat and clear. They will give fresh, reasonable and practical suggestions on how to identify love and put it to use. Ask your minister or school counselor or librarian for a few titles.

Talk to young married couples who seem happy. An older sister or friend might be glad to answer questions and give valuable feedback.

Ask your parents how they knew they were in love. What have they learned about love? Check with your grandparents. Not only is it educational, but you can help span the generation gap. Adults want to share with their young people, but they often don't know how to start. Broad, unoffensive questions will get many of them into the talking mood.

Read the Bible. It has terrific stories and passages of Scripture about love. A good place to start is 1 Corinthians 13. Then turn to Ephesians 5:25 for a perspective on marriage. The Song of Songs discusses passionate married love.

Get to know Jesus Christ. Much of his teaching and life is centered around the power and potential of love. His instruction to love our enemies, love our neighbors, love our spouses is incredibly valuable. Christ's illustration of laying down our lives for the people we love suggests total dedication (Jn 15:13).

Ask your class, pastor, Sunday-school teacher or any group to discuss love. Most groups are looking for subjects to talk about, and we need to speak up and tell them that this would be of interest to us and to other young people. Discussing love with reasonable people will shed much light on what we need to know.

It isn't uncommon for couples to get married knowing nearly nothing about love. Often, one of the partners knows more about it and practices it better than the other (not just sex, but love). The one becomes a teacher to the other, but frequently it is a difficult and even painful process. Too often they don't learn from each other, and the relationship heads straight down the tube.

Learn as much about love as you can before you get married. How often have we heard a divorced person say, "If I get married again, I'll do things a lot differently." This person has learned about love the hard way. It would have been far less painful to learn about love sooner.

One example is Brian. Though his family was a good one, it had a couple of distinctive negative character traits. The members of his family would do anything for each other except touch or say that they loved a family member. Love was "understood" but never spoken.

When Brian married, his wife, Angela, was totally mystified. Most everything went smoothly enough. They worked hard, paid their bills, never argued; but almost immediately Angela sensed that Brian kept a stiff sense of distance from her. He would fix a faucet, run an errand, even go shopping with her, but he avoided any feeling of closeness. He never said the magic word "love," and he seldom touched Angela outside of bed.

In time she discussed her feelings with Brian, and he was shocked that those things were important to her. Over time they made some difficult adjustments, but Brian never did become exactly what Angela had in mind.

Learn as much about love as you can before you get married.

4
Why Are We Afraid to Love?

W *hen we talk to young people, we find that they have* a great deal of fear about love, marriage and relationships. They know that they will eventually enter into a partnership, and the thought of it nearly turns them to stone.

If you met Diane, you could see the apprehension in her face. She was suffering from "yo-yo" relationships. Diane would meet someone, go on a couple of dates and find a way to end it. The dates were fun, the guy was a charmer, but she was afraid of the risk.

Diane was willing to take the chance of meeting someone, but she couldn't stand the pressure of getting to know another. She could toss the yo-yo out, but too soon she would give it a yank and pull it back in.

All of this sounds innocent enough. Everyone has a right to operate his own yo-yo. The problem with Diane was that this had become a pattern. It was time to ask herself if she was afraid of something.

Fear is not completely unreasonable. We all read the statistics. Marriages frequently fall apart, and the pain of broken relationships is devastating. The many "shipwrecks" leave young people reluctant to book passage. Fortunately, reluctance usually gives way to enthusiasm, and most people eventually climb aboard. That's great! There are millions and millions of untold stories about happy couples who make their marriages fulfilling and rewarding.

Given the bad publicity that love is receiving, the massive apprehension is not surprising. Since fear plays such a large role for those who avoid serious, lasting relationships, we should stop to identify a few of the biggies. Five big fears need to be recognized, identified and handled. Check these out and see if any or all of them are true of your situation.

Fear of Making Decisions

If there are three or four huge decisions to process in life, love has to be near the top. Choosing a partner has to put our nerve endings on edge and send our brain waves racing. We are talking about normal fright. This doesn't make us strangers in the human race. Decision making is tough, and it is often even tougher when the stakes are high. Even people who make executive decisions daily and rapidly often find decision making tough. There is nothing like it.

Lana was a girl who had no trouble making decisions. In January she decided to marry Allen. In February she decided not to marry Allen. In March Lana again decided to marry Allen, but then April rolled around. Lana could make decisions left and right; her problem was sticking with one.

We may need to remind ourselves of a few guidelines.

1. Decision making is a gift from God.

One of the marks of human dignity is that we have decisions to make. It is both an honor and reaffirmation of our worth that we are able to choose. Accept it with thanksgiving.

2. Decision making is an act of freedom.

If we put off making a selection, we can become the prisoner of indecision. When I need another car, I spend a long time listening to engines hum and kicking tires. At first it's entertaining to pick over the litter. But after many days of weighing my options, the load of decision making becomes a burden.

I will be able to get on to the next stage of a satisfying life by casting my lot and enjoying my choice.

3. Decision making is a launching pad.

Indecision prevents us from entering a new avenue of love and happiness. There is a door which must be opened, and only I have the key. No one else should turn it for me.

Fear of Losing Control

There is no way to catch fish and still keep the worms. At some point they must be cast out into the water.

If I choose to love, I must toss myself out and take some risks. Anyone who is dedicated to remaining totally in control will miss the pleasure of sharing a life with someone.

When control becomes too big of an issue, we become its slave. The very freedom we clamor for turns into a dictator.

The biblical principle goes this way: "He who saves his life will lose it." Jesus applied this principle to discipleship, but the same measurement is true of relationships. If we hold ourselves back, we rob our union of vital love.

Christ has taught us to love God with "all your heart" (Mk 12:33). Spontaneously and totally is the only way to love with commitment.

Too many people love someone because they have a need to exercise power over others. Their love concept is twisted. Their real need is to control others. They are not about to lose control, and they see a relationship as another way to gain an advantage.

This thirst for power is not love. If you are becoming involved with such a person, step back and take a second look. Not many healthy people need a person to run their lives. Promise yourself that you will protect your distance until you are positive that this person is reasonably free from the dominance struggle.

Fear of Intimacy

When Peggy was in college, her roommates always scared her to death. She was constantly afraid they would discover her bad habits. Each day Peggy straightened up her desk, picked up her stuff and was as polite as she could be. At night and in the morning she would steal away into her closet to change clothes.

Daily, Peggy was afraid her roommates would get to know her too well. After all, she reasoned, if people get to know me, they will dislike me.

With such an overwhelming fear of intimacy, Peggy is bound to find it difficult to open up and share with someone she loves. And she knows it. That is why she stands at arm's distance from every male. Peggy has the mistaken notion that to know her well is to dislike her. Little does she understand that there is a man somewhere who could love her down to her Nikes.

Men appear to have a particular problem with intimacy. More concerned with keeping their guard up, more fearful of showing their emotions, they feel a need to protect their space. Many seem to think that manhood must maintain a sense of mystery. As long as they are not completely known, they can try to support the myth that men are superior.

This isn't entirely the fault of men. Often, society in general—and some women in particular—want men tight-lipped and distant.

The ability to accept intimacy will enhance both our physical and spiritual lives. Job could reminisce of happier times "when God's intimate friendship blessed my house" (29:4).

Intimacy is worth the risk. Someday you will be glad that a loving individual knows you that well.

Fear of Good Things

Have you ever had the feeling that a level-headed, caring person in your life would be more than you deserve? I meet people with this hang-up. They marry an alcoholic, or someone perpetually unemployed, or a gambler or an abuser, and they believe they deserve such a person. If that sounds ridiculous, count yourself fortunate. For too many this seems perfectly logical.

Their reasoning goes in this vein: Their view of love suggests that they need to find someone who is highly dependent and then become the nurturer of this person. They confuse love with helping the down-and-out person. That kind of help might be great if you were running a soup kitchen or a halfway house, but it makes a terrible love relationship. Often the person did not just stumble into a poor relationship but actually sought one. Unable to accept an equal relationship, this person wanted to be desperately needed.

Each of us is more valuable than this. If you want to help the downcast, work in the city mission. But if you want to love someone, find an equal who will love in return.

Fear of Failure

What happens if we choose to love and admit it? What if we actually say "I love you" or merely feel that way deep inside? Is love too much of a commitment for us to risk?

Everyone who chooses to love casts a vote for hope. They mark the ballot that says they are pro-optimism. Even though there are many pitfalls and obstacles, they decide to give happiness a shot. Because they dare to take the challenge, there are millions and millions of extremely happy couples.

If fear is to paralyze us, there will be no joy in life. Take your best opportunity, and ask God to send his Spirit into your relationship. Give your best dream a chance to find the break of day.

5

A Need
to Love
Someone

■ The first principle of love is to find someone to love.
■ The second principle of love is to find someone to love us.
■ The third principle of love is that we love each other equally.

Human love is a tricky business. We lack a good definition of love. We are short on adequate role models for love. And we confuse love with selfishness, lust and personal gain.

With this feeble footing, it's no wonder we come at love from the wrong direction. Relationships and marriage are often established backwards from the very beginning.

Charlie is a prime example. He wanted to date a girl who would look good by his side, who would help him with geometry and kiss when he wanted. Charlie's concept of love was to find a person who would both enhance his appearance and be available for services.

Not that Charlie was mean or totally thoughtless. He was willing to pay for the amenities. Dinner, an occasional movie, a night at the auto races . . . they were all part of what he expected to provide.

That was Charlie's concept of love.

Before we are too hard on the old chap, recognize that he is a product of his society. Many of us share this weak view of love. To begin with, Charlie probably doesn't know any better; but he might do better if he were taught how to feel and behave.

Finding Someone to Love

This is the first principle of life. Many of us drown by asking the wrong question first. We want to know who in the world loves us. Some people ask that question day and night. When they can't convince themselves of the correct answer, they sit and pout.

That's understandable. Once in a while it happens to most of us. But this could mean that we have our priorities out of order.

Find some people to love. Become concerned about the neighbor's child and be his "cookie person." Adopt a lonely person your own age and gently lead her out of the shell she hates. Collect a new friend and care about that person's interests and goals. Look for ways to help the people you already know. Begin to love an enemy (Mt 5:44).

By loving others we put ourselves in the position to receive love. A loving person is easier to love.

"This is the message you heard from the beginning: We should love one another" (1 Jn 3:11).

When looking for a lasting relationship—a boyfriend, a girlfriend, a marriage partner—be sure you do or could love that person. That isn't as silly as it might sound. Millions of people marry partners they do not love. Often they rationalize:

1. I will grow to love her.

2. Love is overrated.

3. Love is not practical.

4. We share interests in other things.

5. Sex is enough without love.

6. It's more important to escape my parents.

We must genuinely enjoy being with the person. We must share and appreciate her value system. We must like to do things for him as well as with him.

Everyone should meet Judy. She has been married for five years to Brent. He climbs telephone poles for a living, and she works part-time in a realty office. Ask her if she has a good marriage and Judy grins. Ask why and she centers on the subject of her husband. She loves his qualities. Brent is dependable, thoughtful, helpful and has a cool sense of humor. Judy likes to spend time with the guy.

Brent is a person Judy loves being around. That's why she decided to be around him all the time.

Finding Someone to Love Us

Shirley loved a man who didn't love her, and she married him anyway. She fantasized that her love would be enough for both of them. Eight years later, with crying children and mounting bills, Shirley discovered that a one-sided love simply can't hack it.

Hang this on your refrigerator door: It is reasonable for each and every one of us to be loved.

Anyone who believes he is not worth loving could be heading for a painful and twisted relationship. That person is inviting abuse and could well receive it.

If you are not persuaded that your partner loves you, approach the problem directly. Talk about it. The leading questions are:

1. Does he say he loves you?

2. Does he act like he loves you?

3. Is she consistent in loving you?

4. Is she mostly self-centered?

Love is a great subject to discuss. It is not a desert flower that closes up at the sight of daylight. Be satisfied that the special person in your life generally and persistently loves you.

Loving Each Other Equally

The Song of Songs says, "I am my lover's and my lover is mine" (6:3).

Swear to yourself the following: "I will never marry anyone who believes I am inferior." It is amazing how many people get married to be protected, or cared for or watched over. This is true of both men and women.

It is impossible to have a healthy relationship if either partner is treated as a nonequal. Neither party should look down on or pity the other. If you know that is happening, straighten it out or catch the next plane before you hit the altar.

One of you may not spell as well as the other. You probably can't throw a softball the same distance. Performances like that are not at issue. But all of us have a right to feel valuable, important, capable, trustworthy and a carload of other attributes.

Love someone who will accept and support your sense of equal worth.

6
Where Can You Find Love?

F*inding love is important. As children we made up* games like pulling the petals off flowers and repeating, "He loves me, he loves me not." Whichever we said as we held the last petal was supposed to determine whether or not the person in question actually loved us.

Women in England at one time pinned five bay leaves to their pillows on Valentine's Day Eve. One leaf was attached to each corner and one in the middle. As each woman slept that night, she expected to dream of the man she was to marry. Men were sometimes less subtle. They used to meet with a group of friends and draw the names of young women. They were then expected to pin her name to their sleeve and wear it for the next few days. From that bold practice we may have gotten the phrase "wearing your heart on your sleeve."

Our modern attempts to find "the" person aren't much better. Frustrated, some of us simply turn the entire process over to God and ask him to tend to the details. While we need to ask God for guidance, we ask a bit much if we expect our Heavenly Father to do all the work. God gives us milk, but he expects us to make the pudding. God gives us the capacity to love, but he leaves it up to us to make the contacts and see them through.

While he appears eager to help, none of us can lie back and wait for it to happen. Love is not a spectator sport. Love is like a shower. No one ever got clean by watching one.

Where Did You Leave Love?

Where can you find love? is an easy question. No need to make it complicated. Love is like an Easter egg. You will find love where you left it.

Occasionally love comes unexpectedly. But seldom does love come uninvited. Easter eggs aren't really left by bunny rabbits. The picture defies our imagination.

Try this logic:
A rabbit
brings a hard-boiled
painted egg
from a chicken
and leaves it in your backyard.
The scenario stretches an adult's credulity.

Easter eggs appear in backyards because someone places them there. Only then can we find the eggs and play games.

We are most likely to "find" love if we put it there in the first place. By showing people love we attract love. If we shell out fear, rejection and distrust, we attract those also.

After searching the house over for her purse, my wife will suddenly announce: "I found it."

"Where was it?" I ask.

"Where I left it," she shrugs.

No one can argue against that kind of logic.

Prince-on-White-Horse Love

This is a cool idea. Someday you will be sitting on the patio thumbing through *Brides Are Us* when suddenly you hear hoofbeats on your driveway. Blushing, you look up to see a handsome prince (or princess) on a gorgeous horse with an extra stallion alongside.

Bounding onto the horses, the two of you ride off toward Cleveland.

Not even in the movies. Not even on the soaps.

The feeling that we shouldn't have to do anything to find love invites loneliness. None of us can hide in a tree and expect that the person of our dreams will happen to look up and immediately become lovestruck.

The Love Principle

People who give love are most prone to receive it. Not unlike priming a pump. By pouring water into the pump we make it easier for the water to come up and out.

Thousands of years ago a wise person wrote: "Do not those who plot evil go astray? But those who plan what is good find love and faithfulness" (Prov 14:22).

The best way to find love in others is to put love into them. We bring out the best qualities in others by showing them what good qualities we have to offer.

7
Buying Love

*H*e couldn't have been more than seven, and he was looking for people to love him. His home life was a wreck. One of those typical sad stories. The boy's mother drank. His father found it easier to stay away than to be with the family.

Lost in the crowd of second graders, Josh took three nickels to school one day and carried out his plan. Selecting the three people he liked most, Josh took them aside and talked to them one by one. He proposed an agreement with each. If they would be his friends, Josh would bring them each a nickel every week. They didn't have to do anything else, anything special. All he wanted was for them to consider themselves his friends.

It's a painful story, but it goes on all the time. This isn't a rule just for elementary school. It isn't restricted to second graders. Teenagers, adults and grandparents play the same tough game.

We don't feel loved, and we are looking for ways to purchase it.

The story could be much worse and frequently is. Young people give their bodies away hoping to receive love in return. Adults practically throw clothes, cars and trips at their children, imagining that they can get love with a charge card. Grandparents tend to be wiser from experience, but even some of them try a bit of checkbook manipulation.

We know better.

Everyone seems to know this is an illogical approach. If we took a survey, practically everyone would agree that you can't buy love. But millions of us allow our emotions and glands to drown our brains. Soon we are engaged in perfectly ridiculous behavior.

"I was scared," said Lori. "But I had to try something. I figured that if I gave him my body, he would see how much I loved him. Now he's gone, I'm pregnant, and I still don't have anyone to love me. Maybe I can get the baby to love me."

We see purchasing love on a lesser scale among both boys and girls. Often a girl will set her sights on a guy and start a campaign to get him to love her. Soon she is leaving presents in his locker, dropping over at his house, making offers to pay for things.

That may sound like normal flirting, but before long she crosses the invisible line. He plays hard to get, and she simply doubles her efforts. After a reasonable attempt to grab his attention and get him to react, the smart girl will see the line and back off. Unfortunately other girls will merely up their offer. Determined or stubborn, she does more, gives more, tries harder. She has gone beyond creative flirting and has entered the high-price market of trying to buy love.

We all know stories of girls who have worked for years at "winning" a guy's affection and have eventually married him. They went on to enjoy decades of happy gardening. No doubt about it.

But there are far more sad, dismal stories of girls and guys who have been hurt, degraded and dumped. They were used because they couldn't distinguish between clever communication and bribery.

The repeated saying of "she" is no accident. Men also try to buy love, though, but women seem more prone to the addiction of this mistake. Seldom does a woman ask a man to show his love by going to bed with her. More likely the female will be expected to "prove" her love, and, too often, she thinks she needs to "pay off" for the relationship. The barter system becomes complex, and the woman's body too often becomes a bargaining chip.

Checking Your Wind Sock

When we start going after a relationship, there are several guidelines to keep in mind. Like checking a wind sock, we need to look once in a while to see how hard the wind is blowing.

1. Am I giving in eighty per cent of the time? Have I become the doormat in this relationship?

2. Am I being abused? Is my friend inconsiderate, thoughtless and simply using me to reach his or her goals?

3. After a reasonable period of time what evidence do I have that he cares? How much longer should I try?

4. Am I working off my weaknesses? Do I consider myself inadequate and consequently have to give in more because I am not quite good enough? If you do not feel as "good" as the person you are pursuing, you could spend years trying to pay the person for loving you. Not a happy prospect.

5. Do my friends believe that I'm being toyed with? Occasionally we have friends who are jealous and distort the facts. Most of the time, though, friends are true and can see what we miss. If our friends agree that the relationship we are chasing doesn't look healthy, we might step back and give it a second thought.

Real friends don't want to hurt us. They could be wrong in their evaluation but they should not be ignored.

6. Can I draw a line and say at this point I will quit? It sounds cold and computerized, but even love calls for some rational behavior. If he doesn't begin to show sincere interest in three more weeks, I'm history. I'm going to suggest one or two more dates to him, but the third will be absolutely his initiative or I'm a ghost. That will be hard to stick to, but one-sided relationships quickly turn sick.

Each of us has a right to expect love to do something. If the person you are going after cares, he must eventually show it. He should show love in a reasonable and sane manner. If he gives no evidence that he cares, you need to tell him good-bye.

You may have a great aunt in Pismo Beach who never writes, calls or sends baseball cards. Your aunt may love you immensely but never show it. Maybe. But boyfriends and girlfriends do not operate that way. Love must show itself without being bought.

Self-Respect

Women have become more aggressive in this relationship. There's nothing wrong with that, as long as it is accompanied with self-respect. No boy and no girl is going to give you self-respect. You can't buy it, rent it or leave it. Self-respect begins inside, bubbles up into your shoulders and trickles down through your fingertips. It's internal. No amount of dates, geeks, nerds or jocks will ever be able to deliver self-respect.

They can't give it to you, but they can help take it away. If you work hard at buying love, you can soon feel like last week's lunch.

Samson and Delilah

There is a huge difference between showing love and buying love. In the story of Samson and Delilah the difference became muddy and Samson was hurt terribly. He had a gigantic ego, and, if his friends knew how to use him, Samson became easily twisted.

When Delilah wanted to know the secret to his strength, she used the old line, "If you really loved me, you would do this for me." Delilah knew what she was doing. She explained to Samson how he could buy her love. Tell her the secret and he would receive more love.

This was not the first time Samson fell for this proposition. His first wife had used it to get him to tell her the answer to a riddle (Judg 14:16).

A price had been placed on love, and Samson was willing to pay it. When nothing else could extract the secret, a promise of love fried his brain (Judg 16:15). Soon Samson was captured and blinded. Not long afterwards he was dead.

Buy or Show

Samson tried to buy love and not show it. Delilah was there to set the price.

The difference is clear. If someone buys a flower and takes it to a girl, he shows his love. Nothing wrong with that. But if she sets the price and demands that he bring her a flower, he is being asked to buy love. In either case he gives her a flower, but the purpose of the flower is tremendously different.

If she kisses him goodnight, that might be one beautiful moment. But when he says, "If you loved me, you would give me a kiss," the same action turns into a threat. Love never operates well under coercion. Back off.

Unfortunately some extremely nice people have grown up being threatened continuously by their parents. Having watched that for fourteen or eighteen years, they honestly believe that you get love by wheeling, dealing and applying pressure. Some of these victims can be taught the real meaning of love, but don't count on it. Most people do not change easily.

It should be perfectly natural to show love. We are polite, considerate, helpful and all those goodies. It's pure nonsense to ever try to buy love.

Every woman should meet a man like Bob. He was a decent person.

Not too sugary, not too rough. Mr. Middle Class. The sturdy type. Bob loved a girl named Jan. Jan had fallen off a truck a few years before, injured her back and still had trouble walking. Stairs were shaky for her, and she hated to get bumped in a crowded hall.

Whenever he could, Bob met Jan at the school door and walked by her side. He carried her books and no one laughed. Whenever he could, he walked Jan to her next class and then hurried on to his own.

Bob had his hang-ups like most teenagers, and naturally his glands were running wild. But Bob never tried to take advantage with his kindness. He was not manipulating Jan. He had simply learned at an early age how to show his love to someone he cared for.

After a year they went their separate ways, but for a while they had loved each other in a deep, genuine sense. The old biblical war-horse David seems to have been in trouble half the time. He had an enemy under every rock and a jealous general behind every bush. In all of his difficulties, though, David was thankful that God kept showing his love. He knew that if God was willing to show his love, then God must really love him.

"Praise be to the Lord, for he showed his wonderful love to me" (Ps 31:21).

8
Love Isn't Afraid to Open Up

*W*hen we first begin to date, we go to a great deal of trouble trying to show that person how interesting we can be. Hoping to keep most of ourselves hidden, we barely crack open the door to our lives and let our dates get a highly controlled peek at us. This is unknown territory, so we work with gentle caution.

But suppose the dating continues and your interest in this person starts growing. Before too long you even begin to wonder if this could be the real thing. Now you need to start opening the door and letting this special person see the real you. That sounds simple but it isn't. You want to encourage someone to love you, and yet you want to hide behind the door at the same time.

Experience at Hiding

We aren't likely to swing open the door and shout, "Here I am, baby; come and get to know me." While a few of us can do that, most of us have spent years hiding. We have hidden behind our mother's skirt, behind couches, behind school desks, behind masks (both real and imaginary), behind jokes, behind almost anything which could serve as a buffer zone so others would not totally get to know us. Diligently we practiced, manipulated and studied new ways to remain at least partially hidden. With years of experience and training, are we now able to stop hiding from others? Not easily, but a new openness and transparency is possible.

A change is essential. The more you get to know each other the more you are able to love. The more you burrow into the ground the less someone else can appreciate you.

Imagine yourself as a great painting. You are a work of art. God has carefully created you on canvas with a full array of color, shades and contrasts.

Now imagine a curtain hanging over the painting. The curtain has been drawn until it covers eighty percent of the canvas. We can see enough of the painting to know it has great value. We see a hint of the genius which was put into the work. If only the curator would open the curtain fully, we know we could love it more.

What Are We Afraid Of?

Each of us tries to hide for our own peculiar reasons. Briefly let's look at a few of the most popular fears which drive us underground and keep us from making friends.

■ Afraid we are evil

All of us have some horrendous thoughts and have probably committed at least a handful of dastardly deeds.

■ Afraid we are empty

Sometimes we see ourselves as boring, talentless, unable to maintain an intelligent conversation.

■ Afraid we are inadequate

We keep shrinking back because we don't want others to know we are poor bowlers or poor tennis players or we don't remember much trivia.

■ Afraid we are ugly

Busy hiding the warts, we also manage to cover up our good side. We concentrate on our tics and quirks.

■ Afraid of being afraid

If we let someone get close, he may see our mask of bravado and realize how fragile we actually are.

■ Afraid of our shame

Some of us suffer from floating shame. We are uneasy and embarrassed with who we are . . . even when we aren't sure why.

■ Afraid of our weaknesses

We may have a bent toward gossip or vengeance, or we lie a little to cover up. Under close scrutiny we are bound to be found out.

■ Afraid of imperfection

The desire for perfection is a hard façade to keep tacked up. We don't want to be caught with our wall sagging.

■ Afraid to be different

Our tastes and interests run counter to the average persons. Anxious to please, we pretend to appreciate whatever the group declares as appropriate.

These and others are normal, common anxieties which cause us to control the door and hide behind it. You might add others that are more peculiar to your heart. But most of us have them. We should not be bewildered that we want to hold some things back.

The Need to Withhold

This is no call to let it all hang out. Love is not based on knowing every detail, mood, fantasy and palpitation. There are certain pieces of the puzzle which we cannot find ourselves, let alone reveal to someone else. We could spend years trying to understand why he hated his third-grade teacher and never be any the wiser for it. Maybe he simply disliked plaid skirts.

Some things are not known, and some are not worth knowing. To withhold your love until you do a profile of his eccentric aunt in Albany is to overanalyze.

If we know enough to love, we are willing to risk the rest. The remaining parts of the puzzle could be a joy to assemble.

Never Love a Ghost

Kim went to the other extreme. She met Ken at a youth group and soon gave him her heart. He arrived at meetings and functions, took her out afterwards and drove her home. That was most of what she knew about him. It was as though he had no beginning and no end.

Ken told her roughly what he did for a living and described vaguely where he lived, but she never saw either. As Kim felt herself growing in love, she realized that she was giving her heart to a man who barely existed.

There were too many missing parts. Too much was kept under wraps. Eventually, Kim pushed for more information, for more reality. Like a ghost, he soon disappeared into the night, never to be seen again.

Not Ready

What if you want to remain a basic mystery? What if you enjoy being a distant character? Then you will have trouble loving and being loved.

As you spend time with another person and learn to trust each other, show more of your heart and soul. The gains are worth the risk. If we drop our guard and lower our protection, we invite love to take hold of us.

9
Is It Love or Guilt?

Robin didn't believe she loved Nathan anymore. The spark wasn't like it used to be. There was little lightness left, little excitement, almost no anticipation.

Often she felt like breaking up with him, but that didn't seem "right." Nathan wanted to keep it going, and Robin wondered if it was too late to call it off. So much had gone on.

■ They had made some promises to each other.

■ There seemed to be an understanding of commitment between the two.

■ Their friends would be disappointed to know they had split.

■ Each had met the other's parents.

■ They had become physically involved.

And there was more . . . plenty of intangibles. Hard to spell out, their togetherness had taken on a life of its own. Carried downstream like a river, Robin didn't know how to go ashore. She could no longer describe her experience as love, and yet neither could she bring an end to the relationship.

Swept along by events which we no longer control, it's hard to make decisions for ourselves. Yet the emptiness inside nearly screams out, "This is unreal."

How can you get out of the flow and think it over rationally? How do you find dry land and ask God to give you a clear head? It's a courageous act to take time out and ask what is going on.

Handling Guilt

Don't let guilt handle you. Guilt can be a constructive force. We might feel bad about the way we have conducted our relationship, and we have reason to be disappointed. Maybe we have made promises which we should not have made. Now we must choose whether to keep those promises and cause further damage or cancel those promises and reduce the injury.

On a perfect evening a couple insisted that they would love each other forever. They said it and they meant it. But as time went by they grew to know each other better and to know themselves better, and they drifted apart. She no longer believed she loved him, but she didn't know what to do.

She had a dilemma. To break her promise of undying love seemed like a violation of everything she held sacred. But to commit her life to a man she did not love seemed equally devastating. Absent of love, could she afford to proceed and hope the love would follow later?

Many such couples have doggedly held on and married. Some of those relationships blossomed, but others failed to take root. This is a gamble and a huge one at that.

Head for Higher Ground

Whatever she does at this point will be painful and dangerous. She either has to grit her teeth and try to make it work or grit her teeth and find the best way out.

Will she admit her mistake and break her promise, or will she deny her mistake and risk terrible tragedy?

While the Bible encourages us to keep our promises, we are also reminded that two wrongs do not make a right. To make a binding promise outside of marriage was hasty and exaggerated. The best route now might be to apologize and reverse the decision. That reversal would be the higher ground.

It isn't always wrong to change our minds. If I said I was going to bring suit against you and later chose not to, you are not likely to be angry with me. If I were to change my mind and no longer love you, you would not want me to pretend love. You would want to be informed about my new set of feelings. I owe you that.

We do a disservice by making a brash promise. We dare not cause further injury by pretending to be in love.

This was a vow that should not have been made. It was not made as a marriage vow but was exchanged between two lovers with all the hyperbole young lovers make. You are guilty of saying too much at the wrong time. Acknowledge the fact that you were naive and romantic to give that promise. Wish the other person God's blessing, and ask for forgiveness. Having concluded that you're not in love, do the person a favor and leave.

But What Will Your Friends Think?

Probably very little. They may be sad, bewildered, sometimes even angry at first, but that will pass. Far above their consideration is the need to be fair with yourself and the person you have been involved with.

Friends and relatives heal quickly.

What If You Were Involved Physically?

Most couples have a way of becoming involved physically and sexually. In the past some couples felt they "had" to get married if they had intercourse, but others felt obligated for less than that.

Fortunately, fewer of us respond that way today. If we made a mistake and had sex, it would be foolish to turn that into a forty-year mistake. The fact that you shared sex does not mean you are sharing love.

If the two of you do not love each other, confess your sex as sin and call off the relationship. Don't let the physical relationship act as a lock if you know it should come to an end.

God promises us cleansing if we will ask for forgiveness. "If we confess our sins, he is faithful and just and will forgive us our sins and purify us from all unrighteousness" (1 Jn 1:9).

The act of confession takes care of our guilt. Don't pretend to love the person simply because you continue to feel guilty. Recognize love and guilt as two separate things.

The old concept of "I must do right by her because I had sex with her" is terribly dangerous. Handle love as one entity and guilt as another.

Feeling Indebted

Love based on obligation ceases to be love. If we are indebted, we may want to find another way to pay that person back. But we should never try to fake love or to manufacture love because we owe a person gratitude or allegiance.

After going with Rich for two years Lisa felt that she owed something to him. She reasoned that she had taken up his time and given him hope that they might marry. How could she then, Lisa wondered, dump him after all that?

If Lisa married Rick out of a twisted sense of obligation, she would do him the ultimate injury. Love is unlikely to grow in the soil of indebtedness.

10
Love Is Saying "No"

I love him and I would do anything for him" is the kind of statement you like to hear. It sounds as though she has found the man of her dreams, and she's running around in a daze. She is dumbstruck, bowled head over heels in love. Everyone should have that feeling at least once in life.

But in a more sober moment she or he needs to sit down and take a closer look at that statement. If we are willing to do "anything," we are in danger of hurting that person, ourselves and the relationship. Once you have the "anything" feeling, take a step back and think it over.

The attitude is great. You want to say how much you care for the person and how eager you are to please him. Who could find much fault with that? In saying this you show you have enthusiasm, spirit, dedication, generosity—all valid aspects of love.

Love Draws Boundaries

One of the things Justin liked most about his relationship with Kristi was her availability. All he had to do was give Kristi a call any evening, and she could be ready to see him in fifteen minutes. Whatever his whim or mood, she was willing to fit in immediately.

"Let's ride out to the river."

"I want to go look at cars."

"Want to catch a movie?"

"How about dinner out tonight?"

Almost without fail Kristi would be ready at her door when Justin arrived, or if necessary she would drive over to his place. Both saw this as an act of love. Even Kristi saw nothing wrong with it. Occasionally she grumbled but little more.

Basically their concept of love was "Tarzan call—Jane answer."

If each sees this as love and they don't hassle over the arrangement, why not let them alone to enjoy it? No problem. If a couple wants to run barefoot over hot coals and call it love, that may be their business. But for those who want to rise up and experience real love, they need to see some of the rotten spots in Justin and Kristi's relationship.

There are at least two good reasons why Kristi needs to change her beck-and-call status:

1. To establish herself as a full person.

2. To help Justin mature.

If those things happen, they will have a stronger, longer-lasting love. Should that fail to happen, Kristi is destined to a relationship founded on inferiority, dominance, inequality and control.

Simply said: That isn't love.

But if Justin thinks it's love and Kristi thinks it's love, they could go on this way for years or decades. They settle for a master/servant relationship and call it love. But it isn't.

The Bible says it clearly, "Love . . . is not self-seeking" (1 Cor 13:5).

Love does not center itself on one person. When the relationship is centered on one, we have something other and less than love. We have self-gratification and call it love.

If love at this point were a coin, it would have two sides. The sides would read:

<table>
<tr><td align="center">Love</td><td align="center">Love</td></tr>
<tr><td align="center">is</td><td align="center">is</td></tr>
<tr><td align="center">for her</td><td align="center">for him</td></tr>
</table>

When one person lives only for the other person, he has perverted love. He has totally defaced himself and said "Only my partner counts." That isn't love. Love says we love each other. Love never says we both center our love in you. Never.

Diminished Love

Imagine he or she calls and says, "Let's go and get a Coke. I want to talk." If you are busy, you have to be free to say, "I need to finish this project; can we go later tonight or tomorrow?" If that freedom of choice, if that amount of respect is not almost always yours, something is goofy about this relationship.

That doesn't mean the relationship can't be improved. This simply means the relationship at this point is goofy.

As of this moment you have a diminished (or small) amount of love and respect for yourself. He also shows evidence of a diminished love for you. However, he does demonstrate an overwhelming amount of love for himself.

How do you turn that around? You change it by adopting a biblical concept of love and altering your behavior to match that concept.

Since he is "self-seeking," it's up to you to draw that proverbial line. Let him know that you are no longer available to meet his demands.

You're a person. You need consideration and advance notice. You aren't a dry cleaner, and you don't give one-hour service.

After you say something like that, you can expect a result. Either he will be insulted, refuse to mature and take a hike or he could realize what he has been like and become loving. If he jumps ship, you haven't lost much. But if he catches on and reforms, you may have caught the prize.

Whichever happens is worth the effort.

What an invitation. It says, "I have decided to go for real love; I hope you will do the same." And you could do it together.

Just the Beginning

Once the first step is taken, the rest could be much easier. You may want to say "no" about your physical involvement. You may want to curb the way he or she borrows things and does not return them. You might want to tell him how late he can call.

This doesn't mean you give up all spontaneity. You can still do things just for the purpose of doing things his or her way. But you are definitely not clay waiting to be made into any shape.

What if the new you leads to an argument? Better now than after you have married. Almost certainly you will tire of being considered second-string. Few people are content with this role forever. Wise people discuss it early and improve their love.

Explain that you need to keep other friends. Tell how you feel about keeping contact with your family. State where church and your faith in Jesus Christ fit into your priorities. Now you're rolling.

While you have no intention of going to the other extreme, you do look for balance. Don't go so far as to make yourself the "self-seeking" partner, but the happy middle is a wonderful place to live.

Take the Respect Test

How good are you at saying no?

1. If you need time for yourself, do you feel free to say so?
2. Do you *usually* go to movies you don't particularly enjoy?
3. Are you involved physically in a way that you would rather not?
4. Do you *often* eat at a restaurant you don't care for?
5. Do you feel forced to play a board game or sport at which your partner wins most of the time?
6. Do you avoid Christian groups because he or she doesn't want to go?

Those are starter questions that might show how free or how restricted you feel. The second test is: If you do stand up and say no, how is he or she likely to react.

1. He acts rejected and pouts.
2. He becomes angry.
3. He tries to force you to go along.
4. She argues until she gets her way.
5. She cries.
6. He withholds a reward.
7. She tries to get even.
8. He stays away for a while.
9. Her conversation becomes rude.
10. She tells others she is mistreated.

If these are descriptive of your friend's responses, you certainly have some feelings to work out. Respect is the foundation of love. Respect begins inside and has to spread to the special person in your life.

11
Looking for Models

*M*y wife, Pat, wanted to remodel some rooms in our house. She began to look at carpet samples, paints, wallpaper . . . bits and pieces. Did she want to go hardwood floors and a beautiful rug? Would she keep the chandelier or get a new one?

It's hard to imagine the total picture when all you have is parts. One hot afternoon Pat walked into a large furniture store and saw a room display. Essentially, the room was laid out the way she wanted one of her rooms to look. She felt relieved to see a good example up close. Her dream began to come into clearer focus.

The couples we know model love for us. Some do a poor job, and we wonder how they manage to live with each other. But most of us know a special couple—two people who seem considerate, loving and thoughtful to each other.

They aren't perfect. Their blemishes show like purple spots on a white tablecloth. We notice them all the more because the rest of the material is so beautiful.

If you want to know what love looks like, pick a caring couple and start to take notes. Love isn't theory. It's reality. How do they treat each other? What's their tone of voice? How do they argue? How do they make up? Do they show respect?

Don't make the mistake of selecting a flaky couple. There are plenty of those around. If we make them our models, we will develop a lousy concept of love.

Pick out a strong couple. See as much of the picture as possible, and begin to create your own concept of love. Maybe the couple are your parents. There are many excellent models among our parents, and many of us don't appreciate them until we're forty years old.

The Christlike Model
If we want to see how love thinks and how it operates, we need to look at the Son of God. Christ was big on action love. He taught us that love is as love does. No mere philosopher, Jesus Christ became a living example of love.

By looking closely at Christ, we learn that love is sacrifice. Lovers give themselves to their partners as Jesus gave himself for the church (Eph 5:25). The goal of love is not to get but to give.

The love of Christ teaches us mutual submission (Eph 5:21) . . . a strong antiwar statement. Couples learn to compromise, to talk it through, to work it out, to reach a peace treaty. We learn it is a privilege to give in. An act of love says, "I don't have to have my own way."

From Christ's love we understand forgiveness (Eph 4:32), not the stingy kind but forgiveness which is freely given . . . over and over again. A couple who experience intimacy will be dependent on their ability to keep wiping the slate clean. Jesus told us to forgive seventy times seven, but he meant forever.

Jesus reminded us to "do to others what you would have them do to you" (Mt 7:12). Love isn't controlled by laws and secret formulas. We look at the people in our lives and ask if we want to be ignored, mistreated and belittled. Or would we rather be respected, helped and appreciated? That ray of light enables us to alter our behavior.

A major reason Christ came to earth was so we could see how the Son of God operated. How did he handle people? How did he respond to adversity, disappointment and anger? How did Christ love?

We didn't get to see him in a marriage context, for reasons known only to God. But we can still apply God's principles of love directly to a couple. By reading about the life of Christ and by becoming a Christian, we are able to get a sense of love as it was intended to be.

If we want to see the blueprints for love, there is a place where they can be found. They are in the person of Christ.

"Love each other as I have loved you" (Jn 15:12).

Concepts like mercy and grace and peace are rich attributes in any relationship. If we have received them from Christ, they are much easier to give to the person we love.

The Christ factor adds a spiritual dimension to love. Without it we have to scratch hard to find these magnificent qualities.

12
Fools Are in Love with Love

*T*he temptation is there. *You are twenty-two years old* and alone. Already it's clear that you don't want to go through life as a solo. You didn't expect the pressure to build this quickly. But the facts are obvious. This looks like a couples world, and you aren't a part of one.

Our need to have someone love us is intense. There are a few souls whose heartstrings are tough as piano wires, but not many. We want someone who cares, shares and enjoys having us around.

After a seminar one evening a young woman waited aimlessly as if she wanted to talk but didn't want to interrupt. Finally, when almost everyone was gone, she told me what was burning in her heart.

"I let one guy get away," she said earnestly. "And I'm not going to do it again. I'm going to marry this new guy, whatever it takes."

She was a woman on a mission. She would either make love work this time or break her neck trying.

With this motivation most young adults will find something that goes under the name of love. There may be many pitfalls and disasters down the road, but they are determined to find something called love.

Don't Park Your Brain

If we become overwhelmed with anxiety, we are wide open to doing dumb things. The person who wants to become popular regardless of the cost is wide open to making lousy decisions. Anyone who wants to become wealthy above all else loses his perspective. Love is one of those forces that, taken by themselves, can lead us to an unbalanced life.

In our eagerness to find love we can't afford to leave our brains in the parking lot. We need to weigh the downside before we plunge blindly after love.

King David is a great example of a man gone nuts over what he thought was love. While walking around on his roof, he happened to see a beautiful woman taking a bath. Immediately his biological bells started ringing, and he had to know more about her.

Was he attracted to her personality or her mental prowess or her spiritual depth? No way. David was dumbstruck by her great body.

Quickly he inquired about her identity. He was told in no uncertain terms exactly who she was and precisely who her husband was: Uriah, the Hittite.

David sent for her. He saw a woman and wanted her no matter what the situation.

He had a sex drive and confused it with love.

He chased after this love despite the circumstances.

David left his mind on the roof.

The woman, Bathsheba, became pregnant. David connived to make it look like the child belonged to her husband, Uriah. When that little ploy failed, the king devised another scheme and arranged to have the husband killed in battle (2 Sam 11).

David let his distorted view of love lead him around by the nose. Everyone got hurt because the romantic monarch was in love with love.

Love Becomes a Fantasy

As we get older, we still have fun with make-believe; only now we no longer picture ourselves as a western star riding in to clean up a lawless town. The girls have given up dreams of being a princess who talks to elves and sings in the forest with squirrels and chipmunks.

Adolescence introduced us to fantasies of love, dreams of walking side by side with that handsome young man or that beautiful woman. Most young adults want the full-blown wedding complete with flowing dresses, photographers, tuxedos and reception lines. They imagine candlelight dinners and midnight walks on the beach.

No wonder we confuse real love with the mere trappings of love. It's like ordering a roast duck dinner because you enjoy the orange slice that decorates the plate. If you paid twenty dollars to buy a meal just to get the orange slice, you might consider a brain scan just to see if anything shows up.

Trappings are no sin. Engagement rings are magnificent. Eating takeout Chinese on the riverbank is fun. Wearing matching sweatshirts can be a kick. Even picking out carpet patterns has its high moments.

But these things are not love. To aim for the trappings is to fall in love with the orange slice. After you eat the orange, you're stuck with the duck.

"It's a shame that Danny and Tina have broken up. They had so much going for them."

"What did they have going for them?"

"Well, you know. That beautiful wedding, and their new apartment was so cute. They both have such good jobs, and they were such a good-looking couple. Everyone said that."

They had the appearance of love. But no one mentioned how much (or how little) they cared for each other.

The psalmist asks the question: "How long will you love delusions?" (4:2).

How long can you love delusions? Moonlight, roses, even violins will last only so long.

Major on the Right Person

There is a school of thought which says, "Find a person with money and you can learn to love him. And if you don't learn to love him, the pain will be less than if you were poor."

This isn't a person-centered love. It is object-centered love. Cars and candlelight are the main course and person-love the side order—if it's served at all.

Fantasy-love wants to be on a cruise with anyone. Real love wants to be with someone special, and the cruise is optional.

Seeing the Grand Canyon alone is not the worst thing that could happen. Seeing Grand Canyon with an insufferable grouch will make you wish you were a monk.

You may want a classy lady on your arm, but remember that some women are like a water torture. The Bible says, "A quarrelsome wife is like a constant dripping" (Prov 19:13).

This works for male and female. One of the saddest sights is a couple sitting at a candlelight dinner with neither talking because they can't stand each other. They were simply fools who were in love with love.

13
Having
Loved
and Lost

There is no feeling like it. To love someone and have that person reject you must cut deeper than almost any emotion you will ever know.

"I barely ate for a month," Joyce explained. "I lost weight; I was miserable to be around. I was depressed half the time. And it still bothers me. In some ways I don't think I'll ever get completely over it."

Joyce had been a cautious person who held on tightly to her heart. A large part of the reason she was so stingy with love was that she desperately didn't want to get hurt. When guys came too close to her, Joyce dodged them at every turn.

But finally she had stood her ground, took deliberate aim and decided to love someone. That simple act eventually had caused Joyce tremendous pain and despair.

Was she a fool to have given her heart away? Will she ever be able to take this leap again? Is the saying true, "It's better to have loved and lost than never to have loved at all"?

If Joyce keeps her balance, this rejected love not only will heal but will become one of the bright spots of her life. But during the first month or two after she was "dumped" no one could have told her that. It's harmful to even try.

When she can handle the situation, there are a few guidelines that could help complete the healing.

First, Accept the Pain

It does hurt when you put all your eggs in one basket and someone turns the basket over. There is no need to pretend you are tough. Agony is a normal experience. You don't have to feel ashamed of it.

The same is true if you have taken the initiative and called off the relationship. The pain may be just as deep even though you took the action.

God experiences pain, disappointment and heartache. He understands that we will have these feelings, too.

Pain becomes more painful if you deny it exists. When we fall down, we often hurt ourselves more if we become stiff-armed and rigid. When we roll with the fall, we usually fare better.

Losing someone we love will hurt. If we accept the hurt as necessary, we will get over it faster.

Cry! Why not? If crying will make you feel better, make a two-tissue-box evening out of it. Carry handkerchiefs in your pockets because you never know when the mood will hit you. At any minute you may see a shirt like his, hear her favorite song, walk past a Chinese restaurant you both liked.

Second, Put a Limit on Your Sorrow

No emotion can be allowed to run amok. You have to put a limit on your unhappiness. Otherwise you'll find that you can't get up the next day. If someone dies, you have to trim back your mourning so that you can go on with your life. When you feel jealous, you must end this feeling or your attitude will ruin you.

As callous as that sounds, none of us can afford to let our emotions totally control us. Eventually we must say to ourselves, "All right, I've gone bonkers over this loss for two weeks now; that's enough. I will not forget how much this meant to me, but it's time to pull myself together."

Unless we want to spend months as a sloppy joe, we have to have that frank little chat with ourselves. The sledding will still be tough, but we have to get back on the sled.

Kevin was a college student who couldn't have the woman he wanted. He dropped out of school, bounced from job to job, turned all his relatives against him and has never found firm footing. The woman dropped Kevin twenty years ago.

He is in permanent mourning.

Third, Ask God to Use Your Loss

We don't expect God to remove the loss; nor are we asking him to help us forget it. We want God to take that broken relationship and bring some good out of it. He promises to do that if we are willing to work with him (Rom 8:28).

On the other hand there is little reason to believe God caused your relationship to break up. God can do that, of course, and in a few situations may have moved in mysterious ways, encouraging couples to split. But not normally. Generally God lets us make our own choices— even when they are mistakes. If you want to marry a pirate with a tattoo of a sick walrus on his forearm, don't be surprised if God lets you.

God may not be in the business of dividing couples who are determined to get married, but God is in the habit of mending broken hearts. He faithfully helps people who ask him for assistance.

When we feel like our hearts are going to bleed to death, we can ask God for a bit of internal surgery . . . and we can give that broken heart to a loving God.

Embroider this verse on your handkerchief. Read it each time you wipe your tears or blow your nose: "The Lord is close to the brokenhearted and saves those who are crushed in spirit" (Ps 34:18).

If we ask God to use our loss, how is that likely to happen? One possibility is that God will make you wiser in your next relationship. Perhaps then you won't make the same mistakes. Ideally, you will learn to see problems early and head them off.

"I'll never get myself into a dumb deal like that again." Carol was seventeen at the time. "Now I know what I don't want in a guy. I don't want a guy who is looking for a mother, and I don't want a guy who has to have all the attention. Just the thought of that relationship gives me the chills."

Carol was able, after some time, to stand back and learn from her experience. The next person she goes with will get a better person because Carol has been hurt and she has learned from that experience.

A second way God might use this loss is for Carol to help other young people through her. She is now prepared to be an understanding listener. Because Carol can empathize with others who have broken hearts, she can help them get through the painful days and nights.

Healing broken hearts is a ministry that is close to God. "He heals the brokenhearted and binds up their wounds" (Ps 147:3).

Fourth, Try Again

The purpose of an electric fence is to stop cattle from trying to get out. After a steer gets a shock or two this four-hundred-pound bovine doesn't mess with that thin wire anymore.

Have you ever met anyone who lost a love and has now become a speed bump? He lay down, quit trying and let all life run over him. Instead of bouncing back into traffic, he dedicates his life to his pain. After all, he figures he has to remember how badly he was hurt. And he *was* hurt.

How many people do we know who lost a love and went on to find a great life partner? How many? A gaggle of people. They have been smashed, tricked, fooled, abandoned, bewildered, disillusioned and spun dry. For a while they even wondered if life made any sense at all.

But each of them pulled up their socks, adjusted their sagging belt, combed their hair and tried again. They chose to take another risk and give love another shot.

One day a young woman walked into a lunchroom and looked around for a place to sit. She saw a decent-looking guy sitting alone at a table. He was dressed pretty well, no fashion plate but not bad. He had wavy hair, and she was sure she saw the slight trace of a dimple on his cheek.

"Nah," she thought, "guys only hurt you and then they fly off to some cheerleader." She began to walk past him when suddenly her feet cemented to the floor. As she stood there for a second, her mind told her, "Give it a shot."

The girl made a sharp right turn and sat down just six feet from the bewildered guy.

"Hi," she said. "It isn't so crowded over here."

14
Love
Is
Responsible

*L*ove *can do a lot of crazy things. Lovers have been* known to miss the last bus at 1:00 a.m. and walk miles to get home. Lovesick women have baked peach pies and forgotten to add the sugar. Young couples hang all over each other in public when they used to think that was disgusting.

Since love is irrational, we can expect irrational behavior. Go ahead, run up phone bills you can't afford. Get moon-eyed and brush your teeth with footpaste. Sit at work and daydream half the day. Love acts like that.

Because love is irrational, it doesn't mean that it should be irresponsible. Irrational means young lovers do things which don't make sense. Love doesn't have to make sense. Irresponsible means we do things that are careless, thoughtless and hurtful. Love tries hard to avoid causing pain.

Irrational Love
Take a close look at an irrational couple. Dustin makes reservations at an exclusive restaurant. He and his girlfriend, Sharon, enjoy a candlelight dinner. During dessert Dustin pulls out a small package and hands it to Sharon. She "oohs" and melts as she unwraps a beautiful bracelet which they both know he can't afford.

Hours later they leave the restaurant and take a carriage ride through the downtown streets. As they ride snuggled closely in the moonlight, Dustin wiggles his toes through the hole in the sole of his shoe.

That's irrational behavior.

Dustin is in love and would gladly walk barefoot for Sharon. Love is supposed to act like that.

Being irrational means that we don't think clearly. We start to run on intangibles like feelings and faith and hunches and instincts and emotions.

Love should act like that.

Rational Love
Sometime listen to a person explain how he rationally loves someone.

"Well, I want you to know that I have strong, but platonic, feelings toward you. However, in the scheme of things I believe your goals and mine could work together with considerable harmony. United, we would doubtless make a great team."

Is he looking for a lover or a computer partner?

Occasionally we hear a parent give advice and recommend his grown child look for rationale. The parent will say things like:

"You might want to wait a few years until you develop some security."

"I'd check and see how long the men in his family live. A wife and mother has to consider things like that."

"Check his bank account. If he isn't saving money now, he'll never do it later."

"Find out what her I.Q. is. You don't want a bunch of dummies for kids."

Parents can be heavy on calculated, rational love. "Make sure this is a good deal," they would argue.

Where's the magic? Where's the dream of two people who will work it out? Love, like faith, must believe in what it does not yet see.

Responsibility

Here is the tricky part. How can love be both irrational and responsible at the same time? Love not only can be both; it must be if love is going to be healthy.

Irresponsible love will say:

"Come on; call in sick. We can spend the day at the auto show."

"I can't," she replies. "The other workers are counting on me today."

"Well," he shrugs his shoulders, "if those workers mean more to you than I do . . ."

Love does not knowingly cause pain if it can avoid doing so. To knowingly hurt someone that you don't have to hurt is evil. To protect and care for someone is love.

Whenever we ask a person to take pain for us because we are being selfish, we begin to leave the arena called love. We are then toying with abuse.

When one person badgers the other to have sex in the name of love, that individual is toying with abuse. Whenever we try to force a person into hurting his parents, we are walking on the edge. Anytime we ask a person to do something which will create feelings of being belittled or compromised, we are toying with abuse.

Never call abuse love.

Watch the Thin Line

When we are in love, lines often begin to blur. How do we know when we have crossed over from irrational to irresponsible? Paint the line with luminous paint so that it can be seen day and night.

If we suggest that the person we love should do something that will satisfy us and hurt that person, we have stepped over the line.

If the person we love swings across the line once in a while, don't panic. Most of us occasionally mess up. We all battle with selfishness. Feel free to correct her or tell him that what he wants is out of bounds and you can't go along with it.

A small rap on the knuckles, and most of us scurry back to where we belong. Don't be shocked if you have to rap them now and then.

What we have to worry about is the person who doesn't think there should be a line. He wants everything on the table to roll in his direction. He continually asks for things which will satisfy himself and hurt his lover.

Get rid of the ones who can't learn. Don't marry a person who is unable to distinguish between love and pain. Anyone who is content to hurt you in the name of love should be recommended for a brain transplant. Any chimpanzee brain will do.

Love will care for the object of its affection. Love looks for ways to relieve pain, not for ways to inflict it.

15
The Big Difference Between Sex and Love

Sex is great! Sex may not be the best part of life and its importance may be exaggerated, but sex is still great. The problem is that sex is so powerful that we often confuse it with love.

Love May Be Sex, But Sex Is Not Necessarily Love
If we get those mixed up, we can make some terrible mistakes and end up hurting both our love and our sex.

No wonder we are bewildered. Look at the words we use. We don't like to say "a couple had sex," so we change the wording. Now we say, "A couple made love." The problem is that they may have had sex and not made love at all.

If a young man sees a good-looking woman and becomes sexually aroused, he is not in love. He has not met her; they have nothing in common. He has no plans for commitment; he is not interested in her welfare. He simply has the hots.

Love Might Have the Hots, But the Hots Is Not Love

A young woman watches a movie and sees a leading man who looks like a Greek god. After watching him for a while, she becomes sexually aroused. She even says, "Oh, I love him." What she really means is, "Oh, I sex him."

She has no opportunity to meet him, share interests or find out what his personality is like. The girl does not actually love him, but she does have the burns. Being sexually aroused is normal. You are a healthy person with all your glands working well. But if we see sex and call it love, that's like running across a tiger and believing it is a house cat.

Don't we all know the difference?

If we sit down and spell out the comparisons, most of us can identify sex and love. But each drive is so strong that it occasionally causes us to lose our minds. Because we are people, we don't always think clearly. We need to stop and add it up all over again.

Sitting in a car, wrapped in each other's arms with your hands on the prowl is not the best setting to ask a question like this. The brain turns to pudding, and after fifteen minutes neither one may care what the difference is between sex and love.

But parked on a couch by yourself on a cold evening with a box of tissues and a book . . . that is an excellent time to study the important distinctions between love and sex.

The Lines We Use

Ever since dating was invented, couples have used the same logic. We twist words and lie to ourselves by saying:

How do I know if I love him if we haven't had sex?

How do we know if we are physically compatible?

It's the same in God's eyes whether we have a marriage license or not.

Brad has had a bad childhood; I will need to prove my love to him.

There is nothing wrong with doing it once.

No one is a virgin any more.

I don't want to get married never having tried sex with anyone else.

If anything happens, I will marry her.

We can do other things but stop short of intercourse.

Many millions of Christians and non-Christians are making statements like these to themselves and to each other. And they are having sex. But they are not experiencing love because the two are not the same.

Impersonal Sex

Sex can be done with a stranger. Love cannot. Sex can be a selfish, demanding passion. Love cannot. Sex can be demeaning and abusive. Love cannot.

A person can look at a picture and wish he could have sex with the individual on the page. We can size up her body and check out her fleshy attributes. We can easily imagine how her body might feel—even fantasize what we might do together. But we cannot look at a picture and love that person. Love assumes we know her well enough to care what happens to her. Love implies an exchange of ideas and an appreciation for her values, dreams and even fears.

There is no impersonal love.

That explains the problem with young people who grow up on a diet of nude photos and fantasy pictures. They are in danger of seeing people as "nonpeople." They dream of doing this or that with the body they see, but the body never becomes a person. If we live mainly in that world of fantasy, without normal human contacts, we start to see all people of the opposite sex as "nonpeople."

When two people get married almost solely for the purpose of sex, they are entering a union with a body and a body alone. If their marriage lasts, it is often because they learned to love each other later. Some marriages do mature in love even though they married for sex. But what risky business.

If we marry someone merely because of sex, love may or may not follow.

If we marry someone because of love, good sex is almost certain to follow.

Is Premarital Sex Immoral?

Look at the facts. Because there is so much sex before marriage, we have the following problems:

widespread venereal diseases

AIDS among heterosexuals

millions of abortions

unwanted pregnancies

destroyed careers

estranged families

millions on welfare

Of course it's immoral. Try the logic in reverse. Imagine a world where no one had sex before marriage. Picture a society where much of the above pain was eliminated. Many horror stories would be evaporated if we held on for marriage.

These problems are possible in marriages also, but they would be greatly reduced if couples waited for sex until they became married.

Premarital sex is not simply an interesting debate over the fine points of ethics. Sex outside of marriage often has terrible consequences.

There Is No Total Guarantee

In a context of love and commitment, God gives the rich prospect of a good sex life. However, because premarital sex is immoral, we should never confuse it with love.

"Flee from sexual immorality" (1 Cor 6:18).

Wait for marriage and sex can be special.

You can feel loved and secure.

You can enjoy emotional commitment.

You can have a safety net.

Sex in a marriage context is risky enough. Outside of marriage sex is a tremendous gamble. God's plan is that two people will become one. That special physical union makes this a reality.

16
How to Tell
If Love
Is Real

The theory of love can be terribly boring. Philosophy defines love one way; psychology paints love this color; sociology tracks love as units having community impact. Each has its place in the discussion, but none has the total picture.

Attempting to understand love, I asked a hundred individuals from all walks of life this question: "How do you know that the person you love loves you?"

In other words, how do you know love is real? The hundred plus people were given index cards, and they wrote down their answers. Almost all the participants were married and had children. A dozen or so teenagers also submitted answers.

One predominant theme ran throughout the cards:

They knew the person
loved them
because of
show and tell.

Both ingredients were necessary. Words meant little without action, and action was weak without words. People wanted to be told, and they wanted to be shown.

Whenever someone specializes in one or the other, the love picture is out of focus. We could work feverishly to show our love but fall short because we fail to say the choice words. Likewise we can talk love around the clock and come up short because our actions do not back it up.

These veteran lovers wrote: "He tells me so and has demonstrated it many times in our nineteen years of marriage. He's faithful and caring."

"By the things he says and does."

"Expression of words and actions."

"She tells me she loves me, and her actions support that statement."

"She says so and I believe her. But mostly by her actions."

"Because she says she loves me, and she does things that say 'I love you.' "

"I know he loves me by the thoughtful things he does and because he tells me he loves me."

Love is still in style. The cards indicate strong feelings for each other and deep commitment. Quite a few spelled out what they meant.

"His love for me does not change when we go through different circumstances."

"She does anything to make my life happy."

"He makes time for me."

"He sacrifices things for me."

"He supports me and my goals."

"He loves the Lord."

"We have a beautiful commitment and trust to each other, and we care for each other so deeply."

Isn't this fun? It's like reading other people's love letters. Let's read some more:

"By the way he gives of himself unselfishly."

"Because of her unconditional love and forgiveness and support no matter what the circumstances."

"Because he accepts me unconditionally—he loves me when I'm unlovable."

"She shows me in everything she is, everything she does, and everything she says."

"He wants to be with me, even when I'm in pain. He talks and listens to me."

"Through the various ways she has 'given' to me: listens, understands, forgives, is tender, laughs at my jokes, corrects me."

"I can look at their actions and see that they meet the description of love given in 1 Corinthians 13."

"She does loving things, she listens to me, and she accepts me."

And a fifteen-year-old wrote: "My family: they tell me at least once a day, and they are very concerned about me."

These concepts of love were extremely accurate and realistic. It was enjoyable to double check someone else's experiences to make sure we were on the right track.

17
Love
for a
While

A few summers ago they met at a camp in the mountains. He was a counselor; she spent most of her time in the kitchen. As the weeks moved on they caught each other's attention. Both of them felt relaxed. They laughed easily and talked together like long-lost cousins.

By August they were staring across the room and smiling when their eyes made contact. When neither was working, they would steal off for short walks. At first they locked fingers to say they cared. Eventually they stopped to kiss. For a few minutes they drank each other in and enjoyed the aroma.

The end of summer called them back to separate states, but they had long ago traded phone numbers and addresses. For a few weeks they exchanged calls. Three or four letters followed. And then it was over.

Time and distance were too great to overcome. A photo still perched in
the corner of her mirror, but she hardly noticed.

Great summer! Great person! But was it love?

Floating Memories

The question might seem silly to some, but for us romantics the issue is
important. In our memories there are one, two or a few pleasant, engag-
ing people still floating around. We knew them for a week, two or three
months, a couple of years. Our experience with them was certainly loving. And, as with all romantics, we wonder whether or not we loved
them.

Occasionally it becomes even more complicated. We wonder if we
should go on with our present relationship, or should we reach back and
try to reignite one of the old ones?

Love is complex. Memories, feelings, broken hearts, ifs, buts, and
whatever—they all only add to the dilemma.

Tie Up the Package

If memories are allowed to float forever, they become unsettling. You
never know when they will pop up again . . . sometimes at embarrassing
moments.

Since the memory is so strong, let's label it love. We will never know
for certain, but it most likely was. Love-Lite to be sure, but love never-
theless.

Say it was love if that's what you feel. By saying it you give your
memory the dignity it deserves. By admitting it was love you neutralize
the relationship. The memory can no longer hurt the love you now have
or may have in the future.

There! You've done it. It was love.

Mentally place that love experience into a box. Put the lid on top.
Wrap a bow around the box. Make it any color you choose. Kiss the box

good-bye if you wish. Let your mind place the box on the imaginary top shelf in the imaginary closet. Close the door.

You have taken care of the question. You couldn't ignore the memory, nor could you live in uncertain fear. Was there someone back there that you should have worked harder to keep? Did you throw real love away and have you now settled for mini-love?

Regret questions are destructive.

Wistful questions from the past are confusing.

"If only" questions are harmful.

"What might have been" questions are crippling.

Wrap up the package and kiss it good-bye. Thanks for the memories and all that. Complete the process.

The package is only a symbol, but symbols can be powerful. A race ends at a particular line. A baseball game ends after the ninth inning. What marks the conclusion to a past love? Put it in the box and say "So long!"

The love we had for a while had no form. It floated. You want to give it a definition, a place and a time limit. By doing so you have expressed your appreciation and removed its power.

Speaking through Isaiah God said, "Forget the former things; do not dwell on the past. See, I am doing a new thing!" (Is 43:18-19).

One damp evening a married woman sat in a restaurant waiting for her old high-school boyfriend to show up. He, too, had married years ago, and she wasn't sure he would take this chance.

Though the mother of three, she felt needed to know. Had their love been real? Was it still alive? Could it live again? Her memories and dreams were spilling over into her present world.

Too bad she had failed to close him out of her life years ago. Now she needed to wrap it up and kiss it good-bye.

Love for a while can be satisfying. Appreciate it for what it used to be and move on.

18
Love Isn't Blind, but It Is Nearsighted

My *eyesight isn't 20/20. Even with glasses I miss a* few things here and there. If I hit a golf ball over 150 yards, I can see it fairly well. But when I go looking for the ball, it's usually 20 or 30 yards from where I thought it had landed.

I can see most things, but I can't see everything. Not much of a handicap. I've adjusted to it since the second grade.

Love has similar limitations. When someone rings our bell, our normal faculties go a bit haywire. We're apt to leave our lunch bag on the roof of our car and drive around town. We put the cereal box in the refrigerator.

That's good. Love has a way of messing up our senses.

The Nearsighted Lover

The person we choose to love has some problems. He might be rude to waiters. Maybe she talks about herself entirely too much.

Little irritations are the smudges of life. Either we don't see them or we decide to ignore them. We probably don't notice that he picks his teeth with his fingernails. Not a pleasant sight. But she's too busy looking at the shock of hair on his forehead, his dimples and those deep lagoon eyes. He could pick his teeth with a comb and she might not notice.

Excellent. Exactly the kind of myopia that should afflict all lovers.

Not only is it reasonable to be nearsighted, it is our duty to have blurred vision. We can't love someone and correct his grammar every few minutes:

7:05 p.m. "You split another infinitive, dear."

7:11 p.m. "Watch those prepositions, darling."

7:18 p.m. "Your participles are dangling."

7:23 p.m. "Oops! Another double negative."

7:29 p.m. "Remember, subject, verb, object."

7:33 p.m. "Watch those past perfects."

Love doesn't nitpick.

Love can use the wrong fork.

Love can sing off key.

Love can forget to set the VCR.

Love can misfold the newspaper.

Nearsightedness is what allows us each to love another person. Woe to the poor creature who loves a perfectionist.

Love Can't Afford to Be Blind

We're happy to miss the small things. You might be able to survive knuckle cracking. The tough part comes when we refuse to see the mountain of trouble sitting exactly in front of us.

"I knew he cheated on his first two wives. We even talked about it. But he explained the problem to me. I know he isn't perfect, but those wives of his were terribly cold."

Some of us have eyes but do not choose to see.

"Sure, I knew he wasn't a Christian, but I figured he would come around later. You hear stories like that all the time."

Too often we even close our eyes.

"He has trouble with debt. He couldn't keep track of money, so he simply charged everything. At first I thought he'd change. I really did."

We become blind to reality.

Jesus Christ asked the penetrating question, "Do you have eyes but fail to see?" (Mk 8:18).

Never let love become a cataract. The eyes continue to cloud over until the light can barely get in. Eventually people are only hazy images with vague features. We then have trouble distinguishing who they really are.

Check the Eye Chart

There's no easy way to give ourselves an accurate love/vision test. We're prone to cheating. We want to pass so desperately that we fudge and give ourselves points we don't deserve. If we call a "z" an "s," we will probably count it good.

The real vision test is this: Are you closing your eyes to some major problems and pretending they are small? Does your relationship have huge obstacles and you treat them like smudges?

If there are serious doubts, find a close friend or a trusted counselor. Tell this person what is bothersome about your relationship, and ask for guidance to help you see clearly.

Referring to understanding, the author of Ecclesiastes reminds us: "The wise man has eyes in his head, while the fool walks in the darkness" (2:14).

Wink at some behavior and let it go. But never flinch at the biggies. Walk into love with your eyes wide open.

19
God Is Love, but Love Isn't God

*D*oes love conquer all?

Is love all you need?

Can love be all-powerful?

In our most romantic moments we like to dream that this is true. If we lose our job, face death and hardship, if our house is repossessed, love will see us through. He has a drinking problem; she has a spending problem; he runs up bills; she has an occasional affair. Love ought to be tougher than any dilemma or predicament. We give love Godlike qualities. We like to think of love as omnipotent—powerful enough to survive any storm.

While love is strong and durable, it cannot cure all. Love may be miraculous, but it doesn't heal all wounds. Love might be flexible, but it can get bent out of shape.

Love has tremendous capabilities, but we are foolish if we test it too much. At some point love can fall apart if we thoughtlessly add excessive pressure.

If Love Were a Cart
A girl says she loves her guy but:

He is temperamental.

He is abusive.

He is inconsiderate.

He is selfish.

He is tight.

He is rude.

He is undependable.

But not to worry. She insists that they love each other so much that they can work out all these difficulties. Love will do its job.

Imagine love as a cart. True enough, it can carry an enormous load. Expecting a great capacity, we toss on scrap iron, concrete boulders, car wheels, railroad ties, a couple of old barrels. Busy piling junk on the cart, we fail to notice how the axle is beginning to sag. We continue to dump all of our weighty clutter on until finally the axle snaps. The old cart couldn't stand up under the load.

We wish love had no capacity limit, but it does. Smart people check regularly to make sure the axle isn't bending.

Never Be Presumptuous
I try not to commit my wife to an engagement without checking first. If someone wants us to go on a picnic, attend a concert, go for a trip, I need to say, "I'll check with Pat and get back to you." Even though I am ninety per cent sure Pat will go, I have learned to ask her rather than take a chance.

Our love can handle a great deal, but I would be foolish if I became presumptuous.

Love might be able to absorb every hardship that comes its way. That's a reassuring thought. But if we carelessly assume that love will support anything and everything, we may be presuming too much. Love is not all-powerful.

Love is limited. Love is finite.

Doubtless you know of someone who married a living disaster. He had the manners of a gorilla, the charm of a terrorist, and the humor of a water buffalo. But she loved him so energetically that he became a teddy bear.

It happens. Once in a blue moon.

Don't presume that love will take care of it. Give love all the support you can by loving a person who has as many great character traits as possible.

Love Is Durable and Fragile

Car engines are designed to run over 100,000 miles. At high speeds, through cold and heat they often prove to be tough and long-lasting.

On the other hand, tiny particles of sand are enough to ruin an engine if they get into the right places. A powerful piece of machinery is also a fragile instrument.

You may love someone who has outstanding qualities. But the little irritating things the person does and says may be destroying this otherwise magnificent machine. Don't ignore the particles that accumulate until they shut everything down. Love may not be able to process all the annoying characteristics sprinkled throughout one's personality.

Since love does not automatically have the power to overcome these irritating traits, we need to reduce or remove them from our own personalities. Any that we can cleanse from the relationship will make our love far more likely to succeed. We cut down the load which love is asked to carry. By making the pull less we are better able to haul the unexpected pressures when they arrive. Never ask love to compensate for something we could have eliminated ourselves.

Love Needs Help

Because love is limited, we have to coax it along. We take out time for love. We read about it, cultivate it, plan, plot, promote, nourish and groom love.

Contrary to popular songs, love is not immortal. Human love can die. Occasionally, dying love can be resuscitated. Rarely, dead love can be resurrected. Love has vital signs, and when those signs are dropping the patient is entering the danger zone.

The question is: Can love conquer all?

The answer is: No. It has limits.

The question is: Can love break down?

The answer is: Yes. If we carelessly overload it.

The question is: Can love die?

The answer is: Yes. Through abuse and neglect.

The question is: Can love grow?

The answer is: Yes. Through care and nurture.

Human love is mortal, not divine. Treat it with gentle affection.

20
A
Loving
Listener

We can talk for hours. Jay and I never seem to tire. Before you know it the evening is gone, and we don't even realize it."

Sounds like a happy couple. And they probably are. Each has found someone it's easy to "talk to." The topics are usually fresh. The person you love has twenty or so years of interesting experiences. Many of the conversations are lighthearted. Some are gripping. Others are filled with hopes, dreams and adventures.

They pass the first test. It would be hard to love someone whom you couldn't talk to. That's a sure sign that there is an awkwardness, and there may be barriers to overcome. Not many of us are looking for someone who will spend the evening with us silently counting the ceiling tiles.

Mutual talking is rich soil, and love is likely to grow well there. But often couples will complain after they get married, "We used to talk all the time when we were going together. Now it seems like we have run out of things to talk about."

One key way to keep the conversation flowing is to become a loving listener. This is someone who hears and cares what is being said by his partner.

Don't Just Take Turns Talking

If two people are in love and they are good talkers, that could mean several things.

- They are polite while the other person is speaking.
- They laugh or frown at the appropriate times.
- They think of things to say in case the conversation slows down.
- They add stories of their own.
- They plan ahead and think of stories they can tell during the evening.
- They are careful not to interrupt in the middle of a conversation.

These are basic rules which encourage a great evening of chatting, light banter and a few serious subjects. Conversation greases the wheels of a good love life. The pattern is: I speak, you speak, I speak, you speak, you speak some more, you speak still more, I speak and so it roughly goes. That's fine. Unfortunately, as time passes the "I talk . . . you talk" exchange will wear out. Anecdotes, stories, tales of unusual feats, even the sharing of emotions will grow thin unless we move up to a higher level of conversation.

Listen to Understand

If the person you love speaks words, you can hear the sound. But a loving listener understands not only what was said but also what was meant. If we rise up to that level of understanding, we create a lasting verbal bond.

For example: I tell my wife, Pat, that I came from a dysfunctional family. To add color I describe how that worked or didn't work. She hears a fairly interesting story about my childhood. Pat lets me talk. Another time she will tell me about some of the strengths from her childhood. We swap stories and get to know each other better.

Those exchanges have value.

But what if Pat hears me and then encourages me to share more of how my family affected me? She then begins not only to hear the words but also to understand the meaning. With practice she also learns when to back off because I am not ready to reveal more of myself.

Pat becomes a loving listener rather than a trader of stories.

When we listen to each other in order to understand, we are paying an enormous compliment to the speaker. We have told the person that he is worth listening to.

Listening with love is not prying. When I enter into the speaker's conversation, she might tell me that she's not yet ready to discuss that part of it. Fine. But I have let her know that I care.

Because my family malfunctioned, I spent a great deal of time at theaters watching movies. Much of what I learned about life I gleaned from the silver screen.

Today, when an old movie is on, I say to my family, "Come see this movie." Naturally they don't come running. In twenty-five years no one has asked me, "What does that movie mean to you?"

Consequently, that's part of me that they will never understand. They have decided to leave that part of my world alone.

If you want to grow close to the person you love, become an active listener who wants to know what is behind the words.

Jesus Christ said this so precisely: "He who has ears to hear, let him hear" (Lk 8:8).

Don't hear only the sound of the words. Never be content just to pick up the vocabulary and the syntax. Go for the meaning.

Guidelines for a Loving Listener

This may not come easily. Practice might be required, but the results could be well worth the effort.

Check your listening for these strengths.

1. Look your love in the eye.

Give her the dignity of your full attention. She won't believe you really care if your eyes are watching another woman walking past.

2. Focus your brain.

Be in the conversation with him. Don't try to think of another story that will top his. Relax . . . don't start trying to formulate your reply while your love is still talking.

3. Be active.

Let her know you are listening. Add comments like, "And that made you angry?" or "How did you respond?"

4. Ask for clarity.

"Now you were alone at this point?" or "I don't understand what that word means.'"

5. Check out the motions.

When he mentions his boss, do his hands make a strangling motion? Does his older brother's name cause his upper lip to twitch? Is she tensing or relaxing? Is her voice rising or lowering?

6. Say it back.

"So you still don't trust her?" may cause him to reply, "Oh, I found out I had to trust her," and indicate that you heard him inaccurately.

7. Be appreciative.

"Thanks for sharing this with me. I feel like I'm getting to know you better. I hope you will tell me more later."

We create a new closeness by becoming loving listeners. In return our love is likely to grow and last much longer.

21
Keep Your Self-Respect

*I*t was a dark day in my life. I pastored a church near Sterling, Kansas, and we lived across the road in the parsonage.

One Tuesday a month the church ladies met and did some excellent work. They rolled bandages for missionaries, made quilts, planned suppers and generally met needs. Edna, Viola, Fern—they were great people.

Naturally my wife, Pat (being a good pastor's wife), was an active member of the society. That is, she was until that awesome Tuesday night when she came home after a meeting.

"Bill," she said. When your name is said straightforward and crisp, you best pay attention.

"I'm not going anymore," she continued. "They're nice people, but ladies' aid isn't for me."

"Now, now. You must have had a misunderstanding with one of the good ladies," I gulped.

"Not at all," she said in an even, deep voice. "There's nothing wrong with it. It just isn't for me. And I'm not going back."

Pat never returned.

Every month their cars pulled up into the parking lot. The ladies filed in and attended their meeting. Pat stayed home and went about her business.

Meanwhile I waited for the deacons to come and get me. I was sure that the church would never tolerate the pastor's wife jumping the ladies' aid ship.

But they never came. No one ever complained to us. They were too good for that. And life went on.

What respect I had for Pat. She stood up and exercised her self-respect. She declared that she was more than a pastor's wife. Pat was a person. It's easy to love a person.

Self-respect doesn't have to be selfishness. Self-respect says you have some of God's peculiar gifts . . . some of God's peculiar identity.

Since God made you an individual, it would be a waste to throw that individuality away and become lost in someone else. God didn't create us as mirrors so that we could reflect our partner. Is your individuality a threat to the person you love? If so, you have something to talk about. This week. Any love which is based on the inferiority of one person is pale love. Rich, robust love is founded on two full people who are free to be themselves.

Not that they are free to be independent—love is cooperative—but free to express their own gifts and personality.

Why Love Dies

The world of love needs a pathologist—someone who can conduct an autopsy on love after it dies, dissecting the body to discover where it gave out.

Until that happens, spend some time listening as people explain why they stopped loving someone.

"He never wanted to hear about what was going on in my life. It was as though I wasn't a person."

"Sure he took me places. We didn't go places together. He just took me places."

"She kept choking me off. I couldn't be with my friends. I had to give up sports. I felt like a throw rug lying around her apartment."

"I learned not to bring up feelings. She would change the subject right away. I don't think she wanted to know how I felt."

"It was all his dreams. His dream, his house, his car. I'm not sure what he wanted me for."

We know that heart problems and cancer are two of the big killers of human beings. The lack of respect and of self-respect must be among the top causes of love mortality.

Gaining Self-Respect

Sounds good enough. Let's all have self-respect. But how do you get it if you don't have it?

This is the starter kit to self-respect.

1. Get permission.

Tell yourself that self-respect is all right. Jesus cut off the crowds and took control of his own destiny when he needed to.

2. Draw personal goals.

As a person, what would you like to do, accomplish or be? It's hard to respect yourself if you're a wet noodle.

3. Learn to give in.

Rigid, self-centered people are just as intolerable as putty people. Love is a compromise, not a standoff. You respect yourself more if you don't have to have your own way.

4. Reach out to help others.

The Bible tells us, "A kindhearted woman gains respect" (Prov 11:16). We need both respect for ourselves and respect from others. People who feed only their own faces run low on self-respect. Ask God for a vital ministry helping someone else.

Self-respect gives us a better understanding about love. Self-respect makes us easier to love.

22
What Kind of Love Is This?

D*ick said he loved the Boston Red Sox. Jennifer loves* her grandmother. Joan loves pink, and Dan is in love with his fiancée. Each of them has used the same word, but they have described far different situations. Can Johnny love a baseball card in the same sense that Mary loves her husband? Probably not.

Narrow it down even more. If a girl says she loves a boy and another girl says she loves a boy, are they both saying exactly the same thing? Probably not.

Since love is a mystery, there is no simple definition or description. Even the Bible concedes that the love a man and a woman have for each other is beyond our understanding (Prov 30:19).

Fortunately, dealing with the impossible will not stop us. Let's look at the different kinds of love which a man and a woman might have for each other.

It's possible to have several kinds of love at the same time for the same person. Strictly speaking, none of them is totally good or bad; however, some are stronger and others are weaker. If not handled maturely, each of them could get us into trouble.

We could do ourselves a favor by looking at this pie and asking ourselves which pieces are the most dominant in our feelings. This isn't a test which we pass or fail. But after checking this out we might discover that we would be smart to work on some kinds of love and downplay others.

This could be a helpful subject to discuss with the significant person who is in your life. Each person could add great insight into this interpersonal topic.

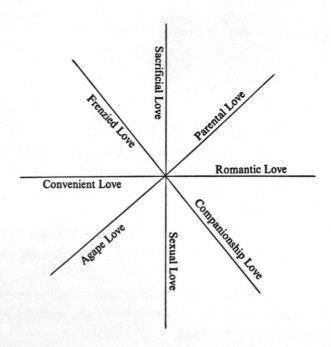

Facets of male-female love

As with all illustrations and diagrams, this one is oversimplified, but it gives us a place to start.

Facets of Male/Female Love

At any stage in our relationship, we might stop and ask ourselves if we are actually in love. Whether we are dating, on the honeymoon or eating cake at our silver anniversary, this pesky little question could raise its nervous head. We can be better prepared to answer this if we have considered its multiple facets.

Briefly, these are what we mean by the eight kinds of love.

Frenzied Love

Do you know anyone who is in a desperate hurry to connect with someone? He is afraid he will be left out, lonely and adrift. There is a sense that she must make a move, and this is going to be it.

"I don't care what it takes, I'm not going to let him get away."

This type of love has value. The person is ready to make decisions and cut through the trappings. Often people run into their second marriage with this kind of vigor. Naturally, the drawback is that too many make a hasty choice and regret it later.

Convenient Love

When you have overwhelming needs, you are likely to fall for convenient love. You aren't sure you can support yourself. You are about to become a pastor and can't afford to be single. You are tired of cooking and cleaning. Graduation from high school or college seems to trigger marriage for some simply because they feel the time is right.

Pregnancy can propel a person into a frenzied and convenient love. If that is the only reason for loving, she may soon be sorry she didn't wait.

Convenient love is risky business. It used to be popular. Trainloads of women traveled West to marry men they had never met.

Arranged marriages occur in other societies and appear to work well. People are wed for the sake of their entire families and learn to love each other afterwards. Young people who accept the system seem to enjoy happy marriages.

Agape Love

When we choose to love someone unconditionally, we take a high road. We decide to love a person in a way that resembles God's love for us (Jn 3:16).

This love accepts a person with all of his warts, faults and peculiarities. When necessary, we forgive each other and remain committed through good and bad.

As Christians we receive this love from the Holy Spirit and pass it on to the people in our lives (Rom 5:5). Consequently, we do not love each other merely on the physical level (though the physical is important).

Agape love gives us an extra dimension when we need it.

Sexual Love

Don't knock it. We were created to be physically attracted to each other. Since sex is often abused, we might begin to wonder if sex is good or bad for us. It's great in a marriage context.

All of us need to be touched, held and more. It's perfectly natural to feel "turned on" by someone you love. If he doesn't get your attention sexually, you might have something to worry about. Nobody needs to apologize for having a sexual attraction toward the person he or she chooses to love. Now comes the hard part because you need to wait.

Companionship Love

It isn't good to live alone. God understood that, and he wants most of us to get married (Gen 2:18). Let's hope that each of us will love a person we like to hang out with. If you say "I love him, but I can't stand being with him," don't order your wedding invitations.

This is the type of love we have for a friend. We enjoy her company. We can talk about nothing for hours. We like going places together . . . all that fun stuff.

A woman recently became a widow. Someone asked her what she missed most about her husband. Her answer was, "Now when I want to say, 'Hey, honey, hurry up; the television movie is about to start,' there is no one to say it to." Companionship love is a winner.

Romantic Love

If you like to send a single, long-stem rose or a special birthday card, if you like to hold hands on a walk, you have been arrested by romantic love. You are a prisoner to romance.

If you enjoy going to dinner at a fancy restaurant or sharing onion rings at a fast food place, you've been bitten by the bug. If you just stuck your pencil in your pop and tried to use it for a straw, you're hopeless.

Not everyone has it. Some couples would rather stain old furniture or rake leaves; but if you enjoy breathing the night air as you and your special somebody walk aimlessly around town, you're hooked.

Parental Love

This one is dangerous. Try not to love someone who is looking for a mother or father. Don't love someone because you are looking for a child to nurture.

There is plenty of room for love in the nurturing or caring sense, but don't become your spouse's parent. We mention this because there are so many people who are looking for this type of relationship. Parental love makes for a tough marriage.

Sacrificial Love

Jill saw her relationship with Mark as an opportunity to make someone else happy. Almost daily she plotted ways to do things for this man in her life. Jill picked movies she knew Mark would enjoy, selected his favorite foods and helped him with the work he brought home.

At the same time, Jill trimmed her own needs to a minimum. She almost never let her needs and desires be known. Jill had decided to find most of her satisfaction by putting her man first.

Every love should have an element of sacrifice. It is more blessed to give than to receive. If we aim in this direction, we are more likely to have a strong relationship.

But we need to look for this warning blinker. If you are the only one sacrificing, or if you give in ninety percent of the time, this love relationship may be haywire.

Becky from Phoenix had gotten herself into a servant relationship. "I felt like nothing. I had to cancel everything for him. He didn't expect me to have a life. He acted like I should wait for the master to speak, and I was supposed to jump when I heard his golden voice. I don't mind giving in, but I couldn't stand being a nobody."

Examine Your Love Life
Does your relationship major in just two or three of the kinds of love but have nothing of the other five? Is it lopsided? Where is the emphasis? Do you have plenty of frenzied love and sexual love, but agape love and sacrificial love are two quarts low?

Love is irrational. It probably should stay that way. But if love totally loses its mind, the people in love could get seriously hurt.

Work on the kinds of love that you think are weakest. Don't work on them alone; discuss them with your partner and build up the low points together. Real love is able to grapple with reality and improve itself.

What happens if there are some kinds of love which you can't bring to life? You are better off finding that out now. It's hard to restore a dead horse to life by beating it. If the important kinds of love do not begin to work in your relationship, you may have to face the facts and make some difficult decisions.

In most cases love can be strengthened by two people who genuinely care for each other.

23

Love-Lite and Commitment

I love you, Rich, but I could never marry you." What's wrong with that statement? Is she really in love with him if she could not marry him? Could her love give her the grace to enjoy life together?

Actually there is nothing wrong with her declaration. She has an excellent comprehension of love even if she can't define it. We can love someone under certain conditions and yet realize that we cannot love him under all conditions.

There are plateaus of love. We love our Uncle Buck, but we wouldn't want to marry him. The very thought of it makes your hair stand on end.

In the same sense we can love Jenny and know that she isn't the "marrying kind." She prizes her independence too much. She hates intimacy. She refuses to keep in contact. Nice person and all that. Great date. Good-looking. A barrel of laughs. But Jenny isn't ready to fit into a permanent, equal relationship. She is not yet the "marrying kind."

Someone can love Jenny but on a different plateau than commitment.

Glued Together

To say that we love each other enough to marry is to say that we want to "cleave" together . . . an old-fashioned word but a vital concept (Gen 2:24; Mt 19:5). It means you will be glued together. Something like a fine piece of wood when the carpenter has taken two pieces, glued them as one, brought them to a fine finish and made them a work of art.

If you pick up a wooden lamp, you can see that two woods have been used, but you see only one product. You don't see one major piece of wood with a second, lesser piece attached. You see the total accomplishment.

This is why we are called one flesh. It isn't a skin graft or a transplant. We unite and become one.

Yet we do that without ceasing to be ourselves. We adopt a new identity without losing our personal identity. Neither of us gets lost in the other person. We come together on mutual ground.

The idea of "glued" love is naturally scary. All commitments have a sobering sense of responsibility. Some people enjoy playing on a volleyball team where attendance is optional. If they aren't busy on Tuesday nights, they drop by and play a bit, but they don't take it too seriously. They like to hang loose. The thought of being a committed, dependable member of the team makes them feel boxed in and claustrophobic.

Love-Lite

Suppose you love someone and you're nuts about being together. The two of you can laugh the evening away, blow straw wrappers at each other in restaurants, sing duets under the lamppost late at night and race up the stairs to your apartment. You are terrific at surface love, and you totally enjoy each other's company.

What you have is love-lite. There isn't anything wrong with your relationship, and what you are experiencing is in fact love. But it isn't all that it could be. If things should change between you, you could walk away with a minimum of clutter. Your separation would be sad and painful, but there would be few chains to break or fetters to snap.

This means you are in love, but you have one hand on the doorknob. Should the relationship begin to shake, you could give the knob a twist and get out of there.

Should you decide to commit, each would have to move away from the door and turn off the exit sign. As a reward for letting go of the doorknob, you will receive a sense of secure love, a sense of total involvement, a sense of acceptance, a sense of companionship and a sense of spiritual unity.

These advantages are found on the plateau called commitment. They are not available with love-lite. Love-lite is hesitant, tentative, conditional, transitional. Love-lite is written with qualifying clauses. We will continue to go together if . . . We are going together but . . . We like each other's company, however . . .

Committed love is full love, and it carries its own list of unique rewards.

But you are going with someone who is completely satisfied with love-lite. Any discussion of "glued" love or full love gives him a facial tic. Or her palms sweat, and she begins to stutter uncontrollably. This person is in love but afraid of what love in full bloom might mean.

Long ago I knew a couple who had gone together for nine years. Bob and Jessie seemed to make a great pair. They never seemed to argue. They would show up at church functions and parties together. They were two neat people whom everyone liked having around.

As you got to know them, some things became obvious and disturbing. One, Bob's hair was starting to gray on the sides. The other was that whenever someone mentioned marriage Jessie's eyes dulled and a pained look perched on her face. She was clearly tired of waiting.

Bob had what he wanted: love-lite. He enjoyed the companionship, attention and even devotion of a terrific person. Yet he could still drop back, withdraw and control his own life whenever he wanted. Bob had no sense of frustration or anxiety. Love in short, nonfattening doses was precisely what he had in mind.

Jessie was far from having what she dreamed of. But she was afraid to make something happen. If she insisted on marriage, Jessie was sure that Bob would run away. On the other hand, if she left Bob, she could become lonely and might never marry. Besides, she really did love the snail.

Finally Bob and Jessie did marry and probably made an amazing couple. But they also might have missed years of satisfaction because of their mutual fears, each probably of different things.

Love-lite is real. It isn't the same as puppy love or a crush. The only missing ingredient is total involvement. But love cannot reach its peak short of total involvement.

Should You Wait Forever?

The answer is: Yes, you should wait forever, if you both enjoy love-lite. But if either person wants total love, then the answer is "no." Eventually plans must be made to do something about the situation.

Decisions aren't easy for most of us. But decision making is a privilege. It's a sign of human dignity. All couples must make choices either individually or as a unit. Try a few simple steps.

1. Discuss the problem with your partner. Before you decide how long to wait, a couple needs to do a lot of talking. How does each of you feel? What are the major events in the near future? What are the hinges on which the door of your future swings? Gather information. Explore feelings.

By refusing to talk about something so vital, you are making a decision to avoid making a decision. Those are usually the worst decisions.

2. Talk this problem over with God. Don't ask him to change the person you love; ask him to change you. Ask for personal strengths like confidence, clear thinking, kindness, a sense of hope, levelheadedness and courage. Commit the situation to God. Be willing to help this person or lose her. Only at this stage will you start to add cool logic.

3. Discuss goals and boundaries with the person you love. Tell him where you hope to be in two or three years. Ask where she expects to be then. Ask if there are ways you can achieve your dreams together.

4. Listen to your heart. Your head is important and your spirit is essential, but don't leave your heart out of the conference room. Never make your heart "chairman of the board," but love doesn't have to be a totally rational decision either. This isn't a business proposition. Listen to the music as part of the process.

Love Becomes Faith

When a couple exchange wedding vows, they are expressing what they believe. They believe that their love for each other will sustain them through the good times and the bad; in sickness and in health they will be dependable, caring and trusting. This means they have faith in their love.

They haven't seen love under all conditions. They haven't had to lean on it during life's toughest hours. Neither have they shared love in life's greatest moments. But they have faith that their love will both prevail and prosper under any circumstances. Marriage is an act of faith.

This is how faith operates: "Now faith is being sure of what we hope for and certain of what we do not see" (Heb 11:1).

Faith centers itself on hope and majors in things we are unable to see. Love gathers its best information, tucks that information under its arm and then jumps. That's an act of faith.

Uncommitted love also goes to the beach. Love-lite likes to stand on the sand, lock one arm firmly around a post by the pier and stick its toes in the water. After splashing its foot around playfully, love-lite withdraws its foot, dries it off and sighs, "Ain't love grand?"

And he called that swimming.

Consider these three principles.

1. Never let anyone talk you into a commitment you are not ready to make.

2. Don't try to force, trick or persuade someone into making a commitment that the person is not ready to make.

3. Don't stand around wiggling your toes in the water until the lake dries up.

24

How Do You Know If Someone Loves You?

*H*ow do you know if you are in Texas? You expect to see an occasional oil well, a herd of cattle, a fidgety armadillo, a crayfish dinner, a large flag with a gigantic star on it and some excellent Mexican restaurants. Maybe a sprinkling of signs saying so many miles to Dallas or Austin or San Antonio. If there is no evidence that you are in Texas, you might begin to wonder if you really are.

How do you know if someone loves you? There are two ways to know. One, there ought to be a gut feeling you have which is magic. You just know it. Every person must experience that for himself. Two, there should be some definite evidence. Nothing mystical or strange about this one. There are signs or marks of love. Without them there is reason to wonder.

Law would call it prima facie evidence if it is apparent or self-evident. You don't have to dig for it or try to make up an argument. Boom! You can readily see that he or she loves you.

Have you ever heard someone try to make up evidence that the person she is going with actually loves her? It happens frequently. She says, "Todd is under a lot of pressure. He is real brisk sometimes, so we do pretty much whatever he wants. But he says things will let up after he gets a promotion. I don't mind. Besides, things will get better later. But I know how he really feels about me."

Where's the evidence? You can find footprints, but they all lead to Todd's house. You can pick up clues, but they all suggest that Todd loves Todd "because he's under a lot of pressure."

On the contrary, she believes that the "other" Todd loves her, the Todd she doesn't know and hasn't yet met. But she is confident that when this "other" Todd emerges, he will give evidence that he loves her.

She's in love with a ghost.

Only One Juror

Who decides if the object of your affection loves you? Sometimes we want our parents, our sister, our youth pastor or our Aunt Rebekah from Arapahoe to tell us if he is the "right" person. They may give some valuable guidelines, but there is only one final juror. It's you.

Ask four questions about the evidence.

1. What do you consider good evidence?
2. Is the evidence twisted?
3. Is the evidence beyond a reasonable doubt?
4. What is your verdict?

Briefly, let's look at each question and see what we must weigh.

What Do You Consider Good Evidence?

Look at three types of evidence: behavior, gifts and talk. We tend to be dazzled by gifts and talk. If he buys you a nice set of earrings and says "I love you," you are likely to become hypnotized.

He sees that as love, and you see it as love. But gifts and talk might not be nearly as important as behavior. Is he considerate, patient, kind, helpful, sacrificing, understanding, tolerant and sharing?

The Bible describes love as behavior (1 Cor 13). We recognize love by what it does and does not do. Gifts and talk are valuable evidence, but they are circumstantial evidence. They suggest that he loves you, but they do not prove it. Behavior is prima facie evidence. If he interacts with you as if he loves you, the clues jump out.

Talk is reassuring. Gifts are thoughtful. Considerate behavior is a knockout.

Is the Evidence Twisted?

In our eagerness to have someone love us we might be prone to misinterpreting the evidence. Have an earnest talk with yourself. Is his behavior genuinely thoughtful and caring, or are you only imagining it?

Some prospectors who found "fool's gold" should have known what it was. In their desperate search for wealth they refused to accept the otherwise clear facts.

Is the Evidence Beyond a Reasonable Doubt?

I attended a murder trial and listened to the judge give final instructions to the jury. He said that reasonable doubt didn't mean beyond any doubt. Rather, it meant, From your collected experiences in life does it appear reasonable that this person committed this act?

Most of us will carry some doubt about whether or not a person loves us. There are fanciful doubts or second thoughts that might invade you now and then. That isn't the question. What you want to know is, all things considered, is it reasonable to conclude that this person shows love toward you?

What Is Your Verdict?

We can't put off decision making forever. Emotionally, mentally and spiritually, do you think this person demonstrates love? If you judge that this person has shown and continues to show love, you might as well accept the facts.

What Is Loving Behavior?

None of us shows loving behavior all the time. We have a great ability to be self-centered, short-tempered and rude. Often we take the other person for granted while we charge ahead, going after whatever it is we want.

Looking for loving behavior means we are looking for patterns, not incidents. How does she usually act toward you? Walking off once in a huff doesn't mean she is unloving. Walking off daily in a huff may mean she is a selfish slob.

Picking all the pepperoni off the pizza once means he forgot. Picking all the pepperoni off the pizza every time suggests he is closely related to the pig family. Maybe he should spend the rest of his life eating in a barnyard instead of with you.

Ask yourself a few questions which will furnish some clues.

Does he pick out movies without consulting you?

Is she habitually late without good cause?

Does he change plans without talking it over?

Does she try to force her way by talking loudly or through intimidating looks?

Do his remarks belittle you?

Does she always insist on her favorite restaurants?

Is he or she acquainted with politeness?

Does he consider compromise a dirty word?

Signs of Thoughtfulness

Behavior reflects character. Character is the quality which will endure over the years. If he shows clear signs of thoughtful behavior, there is reason to believe he will be a loving person for decades to come.

What is thoughtful behavior? These are some of the signs we can reasonably look for. Remember, we are watching for patterns.

He shows gentleness rather than forcefulness.

She enjoys listening.

He is quick to forgive.

He likes your ideas.

She can be helpful.

He asks what you want and means it.

She calls if she is late or can't be there.

He demonstrates patience.

These are reasonable clues but not the only ones. The list could be long, and you may prize other clues as having more value than these. But love does show evidence.

False Evidence

Since we get confused about love, we are frequently misled by its clues. These are some of the false evidences.

He lusts after my body.

He needs you to do his typing.

She is lost without a man.

He borrows my car a lot.

She gets along great with my dad.

He drops over a lot for meals.

He takes me to car races.

She lets me invest in her project.

He respects me too much to pay for the movie.

No! No! No! These are not prima facie evidence. Don't be afraid to pick up love and examine it closely. The real thing looks and acts like the real thing.

God's Love

How do I know that God loves me? Because he does something about it. He sent his Son to die because he loves me. He doesn't simply love me in theory but in practice. God has spent himself in the interest of love.

25
Love Doesn't Have to Win

Bet you a quarter I'm in the car before you are." Beth stroked a brush through her hair as she hustled toward the door.

During the first two years of marriage, Beth was constantly trying to compete with her husband. She knew she would never be equal to him in the job force, so she looked for other ways to compensate. They played board games, took speed walks, water skied. Beth zeroed in on activities where she had a reasonably good chance of outshining her spouse.

She was falling into a fatal trap. Beth was looking for her self-worth through her husband. Her compelling question was, "Am I as good as Terry?"

Most of us have some trouble finding our bearings in life. During adolescence, we work hard at trying to know: Am I popular, am I smart am I clever, am I funny, am I good? In late adolescence many of those same questions linger. Don't be surprised if a handful of those questions still haunt when you're forty.

All that is understandable. The damage comes when we try to compare ourselves with the person we love. *If we have to be better than the person we love, to that extent we bruise the love between us.*

A hard question to grapple with is: Am I successful at what I do?

A destructive question to grapple with is: Am I more successful than the person I love?

Beth couldn't compete with her husband on the career level, so she chose to battle in the personal arena. The tragedy is that Beth felt a need to compete with Terry at all.

Envy Is Destructive
The love chapter (1 Cor 13) says it gently and pointedly, "It does not envy."

If I envy the person I love, a foul attitude goes with that feeling. Envy of the one I love will tempt me to
withhold my enthusiasm
wish her occasional setbacks
rejoice in his afflictions
create sporadic sabotage
distance myself from any victories
keep us from being united
cause me to find fault

Envy will also prevent us from finding peace within ourselves. We will never be content as long as we compete with the people we care for.

The Bible says it plainly: "For where you have envy and selfish ambition, there you find disorder and every evil practice" (Jas 3:16).

I can't think of any way that disorder and evil practice can strengthen a relationship.

Cut Some Slack

Children riding in cars have a way of staying "at each other." One child says the cow grazing in the pasture is black. His testy sibling insists that the big-eyed bovine is really dark brown.

For the next five minutes they verbally slug it out, "Brown." "Black." "Brown." "Black." "Brown." You can almost see their mother's hair turn ashen.

They refuse to cut each other some slack. They fight word for word, color for color.

That's the nature of envy. It can't back off or concede. As Francis Bacon said, "Envy has no holidays." The envious person can't give up or give in.

To that extent he or she fails to understand the nature of love.

Love backs off:

Love doesn't continuously correct someone's English.

Love doesn't highlight failures.

Love doesn't gloat over its victories.

Love doesn't seek an air of superiority.

Love doesn't strut about athletic ability.

Love forgets who earns the most money.

Love celebrates the other's accomplishments.

Love lets the other person finish his own stories.

Love throws last week's score cards away.

Love doesn't keep track.

Love says "Congratulations. That's great."

Love appreciates and doesn't deprecate.

Competition causes us to try to beat or defeat the person we know. Love allows us to help them.

"Each of you should look not only to your own interests, but also to the interests of others" (Phil 2:4).

And what are the interests of others? You'll recognize them when you see them. Here are a few that I know:

■ Bob quit his job for one year so he could watch the children while his wife went back to school.

■ David attends all the necessary social functions so his wife can run for political office.

■ Shirley plays golf with her husband so he will play more often and improve his health.

■ Adrian took care of the children for six weeks while his wife did mission work in Guatemala.

■ Linda took archery lessons so she could hunt with her husband.

Competition doesn't understand the phrase "also the interests of others." But love comprehends it extremely well.

In Love with a Competitor

How fortunate you are. You love someone who is highly competitive and you know it. Now is the time to address the subject.

Take the person to lunch. Sit across from him. Hold his hand. Make eye contact and keep it.

In your best loving tone say:

"I know you like to compete. That's fine. Compete in business, on the athletic field, even have a better lawn than the neighbors.

"But when it's the two of us, let's knock off the competition. I like you best when we pull together instead of pulling apart.

"Boy, do I love you."

Competitiveness is so harmful it needs to be confronted. Left unfettered, competition will drive many couples apart, as it makes one partner feel worthless.

Have you ever known a young woman who enjoyed singing in a choir or other musical group? Have you seen her boyfriend nervously twitching and pacing in the back of the auditorium while she practiced? He looked so uncomfortable and terribly impatient.

After a few weeks of rehearsals the talented singer stopped attending. He couldn't or wouldn't be in the group, so the boyfriend hated being there. Weekly he used his discomfort as a pressure to get her to quit. Unable to join in and unwilling to help her reach her own goals, he turned to sabotage.

As a result she developed a bitterness toward him. The message is clear. If he can't play, she can't play. He flunked Love 101. If she believes he is worth the effort, she can take him to lunch and tell him to stop pacing, stop fidgeting, go away for a couple of hours, and try not to be so jealous.

The Need to Know Better

The easy thing would be to walk away from a fierce competitor. After all, why get involved with a basically self-centered person? Stay with the competitor only if the following is true:

1. She has other qualities that are great.

2. You are willing to confront regarding this issue.

3. He responds favorably to your confrontation and begins to change.

Some of us have such a poor concept of love that we think the purpose of love is to make ourselves look good. That pitiful definition needs correcting.

Look for real love.

26
Learning
Forgiveness

*F*orgiveness is one of the thermometers of love. It isn't the only way to test the temperature, but it is one way. If every mistake makes you upset, if each slip or oversight rattles your cage, if you can still recall every malfunction, maybe your love is cold . . . down around the freezing point.

"But I can't forgive him. Not after all he has done." We won't stop to argue over the word "can't," but if you don't forgive him, love will remain locked in a block of ice. Frozen stiff.

If I withhold forgiveness, I withhold love. Can I love someone and hold a grudge against him at the same time? Yes! But only if I am willing to let my love shrink into a small package.

But She Keeps Doing It

Holly was the kind of girl who was always late. Her lack of punctuality left Brent spitting mad. The angrier he became the more entrenched Holly grew in her bad little habit. Finally Brent decided he had to do something about the situation or he couldn't continue to see Holly.

What Were His Alternatives?

1. They could reach a compromise. (She would try to be on time.)
2. He could concentrate on her other attributes.
3. He could dump Holly.

If there is enough love between them, numbers one and two are genuine possibilities. Love normally learns to compromise or to accept things as they are. When their love is not sufficient to put one or two into operation, they flunk the love test. They simply love each other too little to continue.

Love gives her the incentive to change. Love gives him the ability to forgive. If neither of these efforts is possible, there might be only microscopic love, and it would hardly be worth the work it takes to find it.

The Ability to Forgive Often

Frustrated, we say, "But I've forgiven her for that before." Usually this means that we expected to get a medal for our chivalry. If we forgave twice, we imagined knighthood would soon be forthcoming.

Nothing like that happened, and now we are expected to forgive a third time. Taxed to the limit, we wonder how long this can go on. Soon love is replaced by self-pity.

One of the basic tenets of forgiveness is that we can expect to need to do it again. We would enjoy a simpler approach, but we seldom get it. Suppose someone insults us. We explain how they hurt our feelings, and we forgive them. That should settle the matter. But it doesn't.

Two months later, the person we love insults us again. Our blood boils because we thought we had handled that messy problem. It rears its ugly head a second time.

Love forgives again . . . and again . . . and again. Love is in the forgiveness business.

Jesus Christ said something about forgiving seventy times seven and all that.

Forgiveness Works for Us Too

The person who is afraid to get close to someone will find forgiveness to be a great friend. If love means forgiving others, love also means that I will be forgiven.

Intimacy frightened Angela nearly to death. She didn't want people too close because they would soon discover her failings. Her foul temper, her sloppiness, her lack of patience, her selfishness were just part of what she perceived as her unbearable traits. Painfully, Angela held men at arm's length.

Unfortunately, she didn't understand that love equals forgiveness and forgiveness will cover all of our real and imagined shortcomings. The person who loved her would soon learn that Angela butters both sides of her toast, enjoys all-star wrestling, leaves the newspaper on the floor, squeezes the toothpaste in the middle and can be terribly selfish. The person who loves her will forgive her for all that and more.

What if you have found someone who is not very forgiving? Is that enough reason to question the person's love? Yes! Anybody who cannot forgive regularly has one of these problems:

1. Little love for you
2. No love at all for you

The situation isn't hopeless. Love might increase if a sense of forgiveness develops. But love that knows nothing of forgiveness is unhealthy if it exists at all.

Expect forgiveness. It's one of the genuine evidences of love.

Getting in Touch with Forgiveness

Our ability to give or accept forgiveness is often connected directly to our experience with God. If we see God as unforgiving, we have not seen a good example. If we think of God as forgiving, but begrudgingly so, we are likely to deal out a stern forgiveness.

Check out Colossians 3:13: "Forgive as the Lord forgave you."

What is the pattern? How has God forgiven us? Lovingly, freely, repeatedly, graciously and more.

Take our experience with God, and draw the same pattern for how we will forgive others. If we think God has forgiven us in a mean, conditional, partial or halfhearted way, then that is likely to be the way we will forgive others.

Jesus Christ is our prime example of love and forgiveness. If we can accept his openhanded, smiling, limitless forgiveness, we can pass it on the same way.

The woman who poured an alabaster jar of perfume on the feet of Jesus is described as a "sinful" woman. What does sinful mean? Was she guilty of snoring in the synagogue, or had she lied about her weight at the local exercise club? Maybe she was a ringleader in a camel-rustling gang. Just as likely she was a prostitute.

Whatever her problem, the Pharisees were shocked that Jesus would have anything to do with her. Jesus in turn was disturbed that they couldn't forgive her.

His rule of thumb was this simple: "He who has been forgiven little loves little" (Lk 7:47).

If someone is stingy at dispensing forgiveness, that person probably sees God as the Frugal Forgiver.

The same can be true of perfectionists. They believe that they have everything under control. Because they think they don't mess up, they are intolerant of those who do.

Perfectionists say:

1. I don't need much forgiveness.

2. Therefore, I have limited experience at forgiveness.

3. Consequently, I do not give forgiveness easily or generously.

Jesus says "too bad." Those who have wide experience with forgiveness can deliver it by the shovelful. A perfectionist often has a shallow view of love.

Boot Camp God

I know a Christian who sees God as that great drill sergeant in the sky. He's a good person . . . does terrific work for God. If he had his way, every Christian would be lined up and trained boot camp style.

There would be little room for pampering. No tolerance for error. Everyone would read the Bible at 6:00 a.m., pray at 6:15, memorize verses at 6:30. Anyone who fell behind or failed to muster would be chewed out and harshly corrected.

Despite his deep Christian commitment, this man has yet to see the tender side of God. One day he may see how much God has forgiven him, and then he will be able to forgive others the same way.

There was a man who received a government pension for several years. Eventually, he was sent a letter asking for an update on his status. The government agency carefully explained that if the information was not sent in by a certain date the pension would be reduced by half. When the letter arrived, his wife paid little notice to it and threw it in the trash. A couple months later, his checks were reduced as the letter had warned. Despite his earnest protests the agency would not reconsider.

For years afterwards, he remained angry and unforgiving toward his wife. Because of his unyielding attitude, she shriveled back and found it impossible to love this bitter man.

If he had been willing to reach deep into his experience and forgive her, he could have rescued their relationship. Instead he shackled her with his hate and drove love out of her.

He could have forgiven her this great mistake. That would have freed her to love him a trainload.

Do We Forgive Everything Forever?

Even forgiveness can be taken to absurdity. A conscientious person is dating someone who is an insulting, rude, callous, self-centered dork. As a Christian, should you ignore his every quirk and love him anyway?

No. He doesn't show any sign of love on his part. If you want to be a martyr, at least do it for a good cause. Don't waste your love on a person who doesn't have a clue what real love is all about.

Jesus said, "Do not throw your pearls to pigs" (Mt 7:6).

Never fall for the false idealism which suggests you can turn anyone around. Share your love with someone who is willing to share back.

27
Trying
Too
Hard

If you loved a child
And you gave it
Anything and everything it wanted,
You could actually hurt the child
You loved.

*T*he same principle applies to young adults. *You may*
have found someone who puts your blender on full speed, and naturally
you want to please her. Sometimes you feel like you would do anything
for that person.

You are fortunate. This is one of the greatest "feelings" life has to offer.
But, like a magnificent horse, this emotion needs to have a bit in its
mouth and reins around its neck.

Never give love anything and everything it wants.

If love is encouraged to run wild, it will

steal every minute

sap all our energy
become self-centered
compromise our values
distort our common sense
confuse our priorities
belittle our faith

When love becomes boss, it becomes a tyrant. Love is satisfying, pleasing, uplifting only when we are its master. Love at the helm will soon drive the ship into the sand.

Amy Gave Her All

The perfect example of trying too hard was Amy. A talented young woman, Amy had many interests and seemed to pursue a well-rounded life. But when she began to date Phil, her other concerns fell into a ditch.

It was no surprise that Amy zeroed in on the person who now claimed her heart. Love ought to be a strong magnet. The odd part was that Amy worked at her new love day and night.

First, she dropped out of her support group. Second, Amy lost interest in her exercise program. Next, she failed to re-enroll for night school.

None of those things was terribly important to her in light of her love for Phil. There was no contest between the study of Russian history and her study of a new boyfriend.

Amy's time was now dedicated to being by his side. She baked for Phil, hiked with him, listened to music in his apartment, held his hand at the mall, went to concerts. They attended church and then hurried out to be together.

What could be wrong with that kind of devotion? Doesn't that sound like the typical couple in love?

Becoming Isolated

Soon Amy learned some valuable lessons about love.

■ By cutting off her other friends, she made Phil's love her only source of companionship. Their love for each other began to suffer under the weight of having to carry the entire friendship load.

■ Amy's loss of outside interests choked off her opportunity to grow. She could receive what Phil had to offer but little else.

■ Her search for security with Phil began to produce an opposite effect. As she came to realize he was her security, she sensed how insecure that sole dependence was.

■ Her faith in Jesus Christ diminished as Phil became her major circle of fellowship. She learned that two people hardly make a circle. That is especially true if the other person barely shares any interest in spiritual concerns.

Amy gave it all she had. Life had meaning only as it related to her love for Phil. By such total dedication, she placed enormous pressure on their love. That pressure eventually caused cracks to appear, and before long their love was showing signs of structural weaknesses.

She got an A for effort. If she had held back, Amy might also have been able to stay in love.

The Irresistible Force

The writer of the Song of Songs tells us that the pull of love is as strong as the pull to die (8:6). Death will not be denied. It is all-consuming.

Love's pull is just as forceful, but it can be controlled. Left to itself, love will swallow up everything we are and all we have to offer. Unchecked, love will reduce us to mumbling fools.

To control the irresistible force of wind, we plant trees. Trees form a shelterbelt and prevent us from being swept away. Some of the trees which we can plant are the following.

Tree number one: Self-development

We will continue to seek new experiences which will result in our growth as a person.

Tree number two: Keep friends.

We will not allow love to isolate us.

Tree number three: Moral value.

We will not let love blind and distort our standards.

Tree number four: Personal faith.

Love will not be permitted to drain us of spiritual energy.

Tree number five: Maintain space.

Love gives breathing room. Constant close contact has a way of smothering both individuals.

Each tree should be planted as firm protection against the irresistible force of love. For all its good, love can also destroy.

How much time do we spend merely sitting by the phone in case that special person calls and wants to go to the beach, catch a movie, or just walk and talk? Be ready. Be unfettered. Nonsense! Love is best served if we control our own lives and steal away at appropriate intervals to serve love.

28
Love
Is a
Bug

Let's pretend that love is a bug. Excitedly we try to catch it. As our hand darts out to grasp love, it jumps here and there . . . eluding us each time. Finally, we grab hold of love and stuff it into a jar and screw the lid on tightly.

There we have it. We have captured love and have safely incarcerated one of life's great experiences.

We punch holes in the lid, feed grass to the bug and supply a few droplets of water. Love is our possession, and we are its owners.

Before long we notice a listlessness about this beautiful insect. It stops scurrying around and seems to have lost its appetite. Soon this once energetic, playful bug merely sits on the bottom of the glass and stares out into space.

After two weeks of inactivity this once magnificent creature turns over on its back, kicks up all six legs and dies. The love bug didn't die from a lack of food or air or daylight. Love gave up because it lost its freedom. And love without the freedom to fly loses its will to live.

One of the brightest love bugs I ever met was a woman named Sharon. Filled with enthusiasm and overflowing with love, she met a young man, gave her heart away and they married. They were married only a few months before everyone could see a pronounced change in this once bubbly personality. No longer the adventurer, Sharon would forge out into the world and then nervously retreat home at the end of the day. There she remained with her husband, Richard. Exhausted after working hard, he wanted to stay home, and he naturally believed her place was with him.

Richard chose to cut himself off from friends and disliked getting together with other couples. His hobbies were limited to woodworking in his basement and repairing his car. Antisocial, he seemed to become jealous if he thought Sharon was reaching out.

Week by week the glow in Sharon's eyes dimmed. Soon she showed all the marks of a hopeless captive. The lid of the jar of her life was screwed on tightly, and she was losing any hope of ever flying again.

Inverted and Insecure
Love which must control, stifle and imprison is a love of ourselves and not love for the other person. The person who must have you here by his side, who is afraid to let the other person go and grow, is basically guilty of self-love.

Richard understands love only as it affects him. If the object of his love, Sharon, is encouraged—or even permitted—to fly on her own, how will that detract from what he wants and needs?

Richard might not intend to be mean or self-serving, but he has only one concept of love. He sees love not as something to give but as something to get. He believes in hoarding and smothering love.

Like the little boy who found a baby bird and tucked it inside his jacket. As the bird struggled to get free, the boy held it tighter, because he wanted to keep it. Soon the tiny bird stopped fighting and lay passively inside the child's coat. Then the boy could keep the bird he prized, but the bird was dead. He never stopped to ask what would have been best for the bird. His constant question was, "How can I keep the bird and accomplish what is best for me?"

Inverted and insecure love is too distorted to really qualify as love. It is simply selfishness disguised as love.

Freedom Is Risky

What will happen if we let the person we love go free? He might not come back. He might get into mischief. She might find interests of her own. That is all true. But he also might fly around and come back on his own. Then we will have someone with us who chooses to be there, and our love is stronger for the experience of freedom.

The apostle Paul was practically jumping up and down over the idea that Jesus Christ had set him free. Paul was at liberty to make choices on his own.

"It is for freedom that Christ has set us free" (Gal 5:1).

This is risky business. I might decide to do some perfectly weird things. But Jesus Christ was willing to take the chance with me.

My wife, Pat, feeds birds in our backyard. She puts popcorn on an elevated platform, and a variety of feathered creatures taxi in for a short meal. Ten feet from there, Pat has also hung a bird feeder from a cedar tree. In the winters she packs this with birdseed. As a reward she gets to see blue jays, cardinals and an assortment of other winged friends.

Unlike the boy who tucked the bird in his jacket to keep, Pat would never try to trap and cage any of the birds she feeds. The thought would offend her. She loves to watch the birds that come to feed and is thrilled that they choose to come and eat in her backyard. They will always be free.

Love Is for the Strong

If we are weak or mentally mushy, we want to pull everything in toward ourselves. We are not prepared to see the person we love reach out, succeed and grow. His very happiness becomes a threat to us if we are inverted and insecure.

A husband asked his wife where she and her friend were going. She replied that they were going to spend Saturday in Kansas City, just fifty miles away.

"But where in Kansas City?"

"Just around," she answered.

"I need to know more than that," he pressed.

"Well, if you have to know, we are going shopping at the mall and we'll probably have lunch at The China Wall," she said resentfully.

The next day he drove to Kansas City and during the lunch hour circled the parking lot of The China Wall until he saw her car.

"What could be wrong with that?" he asked later. "I was only trying to protect our relationship." No doubt he saw it that way. Unfortunately he was strangling the person he loved.

29
Male and Female Love

*T*his is how we sometimes picture men and women in love.

1. The male: He is the strong-willed, bossy, confident, silent, aggressive type; a person of few words, he barely grunts, and his female companion shuffles off to make his every dream come true; he is stone-faced, unemotional and mysterious.

2. The female: She's obedient, a little giddy, gushy, a fuzzy thinker, unsure of herself; basically, she lives to make him happy and hopes a few crumbs of pleasure and fulfillment will drop her way.

He is the meat of life and she is the dessert. He is steak and strength while she's a soft Twinkie.

For decades we imagined men and women, boys and girls, fit into these stereotypes. Some of those images still exist, and many young people are busy trying to live up to those misguided patterns.

Let's take a more serious look at male and female roles as we have pictured them and then ask how we can meet somewhere in the middle. Our ability to love is distorted by who we think we are. If we can move away from those false roles, we will be freer to let go and love each other.

How do we tend to see men and women? To begin with, here are nineteen opposites which we too commonly accept.

She	He
Tender	Tough
Indecisive	Decisive
Dependent	Independent
Feeling	Unfeeling
Submissive	Demanding
Hesitant	Confident
Illogical	Logical
Passive	Active
Flighty	Serious
Tasks	Jobs
Dreamy	Practical
Creative	Repetitive
Warm	Cold
Flexible	Rigid
Patient	Immediate
Uncertain	Steady
Moody	Dependable
Sensitive	Insensitive
Spiritual	Material

Read the two lists carefully. Are you angry? You ought to be. The lists are how we tend to perceive each other. They are not true. We know plenty of people who have characteristics which fit in the opposite columns.

Don't believe these lists are accurate, and please don't start to become them. Just realize that it is true that we frequently divide men and women into these categories.

Which Ones Are True of You?

As with most exaggerations there is some truth to these two lists. For a few men, the male traits will fit exactly. You probably have a relative or a girlfriend who matches the female list like a cartoon character.

For most of us some of the characteristics are precisely true. Where this is the case, we each need to try to move more toward the middle. The center means we give up the extremes of our behavior and reach a reasonableness.

How do we leave our "traditional" roles and meet in the middle with more acceptable behavior? Let's try this new list.

She	Both become	He
Tender	Firm	Tough
Indecisive	Negotiating	Decisive
Dependent	Interdependent	Independent
Feeling	Emotionally secure	Unfeeling
Submissive	Cooperative	Demanding
Hesitant	Humble	Confident
Illogical	Reasonable	Logical
Passive	Compromising	Active
Flighty	Fun	Serious
Tasks	Relationships	Jobs
Dreamy	Adventurous	Practical
Creative	Innovative	Repetitive

Warm	Loving	Cold
Flexible	Adjustable	Rigid
Patient	Tolerant	Immediate
Shaky	Movable	Steady
Moody	Understanding	Dependable
Sensitive	Caring	Insensitive
· Spiritual	Balanced	Material

None of us is condemned to conform to the mold. To a large extent we are able to adjust our attitudes and love the way we want. By moving toward the center, we increase the possibility that we will have a lasting relationship with someone else.

Avoiding the Extremes

Couples can take the list and find their own temperament. She could have a trait which is traditionally on the male side, or he might discover some of his on the traditionally female side. Why would the couple be better off trying to move toward the middle with as many traits as possible?

The goal is to reach the middle because the extremes are what cause friction. If one person is heavily illogical or rigidly logical, they probably have trouble with love. The closer they move toward balance, the smoother love will spread.

What if you are always passive or always active? Either is too far out. Shift toward compromising. Any couple who can make adjustments at this loving level has a good chance of seeing their relationship prosper.

It doesn't take a couple to make this happen. We might do better if we have input from another person, but that isn't essential. Pick out your own extremes. Consciously begin to modify them. Change is possible and all the more meaningful if we change ourselves.

30
Liking
or
Loving?

I really like being with Jamie, but I don't know if I am in love with him."

Most of us have met someone like Jamie. The person is good-looking, lots of fun to be with, but we still wonder. We are certainly attracted to him. We seek the person out, sit next to him or start a conversation.

We definitely enjoy his company. But do we love him or merely like being around him?

In the final analysis everyone answers that for himself. Unfortunately, many people get married and then discover that they have answered the question incorrectly.

"I liked her. Everybody liked Sherri. But I never did grow to love her."

That's the theme song of many unhappy couples. They had a great deal of attraction for each other, but love-bonding never happened.

The opposite is also true. A husband will beam and say, "Not only do I like Kristi, but I love her to death."

We seem to know there is a difference between like and love. They are close enough to be confusing. How do we distinguish between the two and make them work for us?

Turn the Question Around

Can we love someone we don't like? If we are talking about marriage/couple love, I say we can't. To say that we romantically love a person we don't like is a contradiction in terms.

Try saying that you love to eat chocolate but can't stand the taste. My mind goes into convulsions trying to straighten out that logic.

There may be days when you don't like her. She could have some traits you don't care for, but to emotionally love someone you don't like is just too incredible to accept.

True, Jesus told us we could love even our enemies. But he didn't mean the emotional, married-type love. The grace of God permits us to love the unlovable. Thank heavens for that great gift. Don't try to love a marriage partner with "missionary zeal."

To say categorically (in the sum total of the person) that you love her but do not like her, I mark that one false.

Can We Like and Not Love?

This is the tricky question. Is it possible to like someone so much that we think we love her? This happens all the time, and many couples wake up to regret it. The attraction to the person was so strong that we mistook it for love.

Fascination is not love.

Charmed is not love.

Attraction is not love.

Infatuation is not love.

Magnetism is not love.

A movie star was interviewed about the men in her life, many of whom were rich and powerful. She enjoyed men who were decisive and could tell others what to do. "Power is a great aphrodisiac," she explained with a knowing grin. Power may be attractive to some, but it's a poor substitute for love.

Suitcase in hand, a wife of only two years stood at the door and looked back at her bewildered husband.

"I thought I loved you, but now I realize I never did. We had some good times but it never was the real thing."

How could she know? As a young bride she became captivated by the superficial, and she liked what she saw. Sadly, this attraction wasn't enough without genuine love.

Love/Like Barometer

No one can tell another whether or not he is in love. The following diagram is simply a tool which could help put love in detectable terms. No one passes or fails this diagram.

The diagram allows us to ask where the arrow is on our Love/Like barometer. Only you know how far to place it. The barometer is progressive. You could be stuck on physical appearance and know little about the person's personality and nothing about her character. If that is the case, you probably like her but have scarcely any idea if you love her.

Let's look at each of the three sections before deciding where to put the arrow.

1. Physical appearance

A person's looks are important. They probably play too great a role, but looks do count.

Normally men are more strongly drawn to appearance than women are. However, looks are high on the list for most of us.

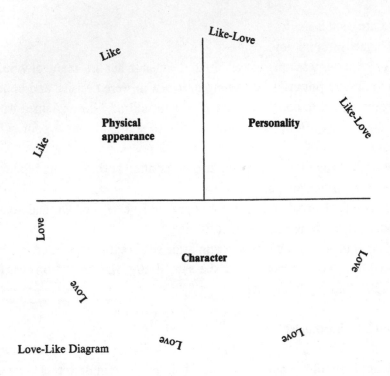

Love-Like Diagram

As we mature, appearance becomes less significant and we search for more lasting qualities. One survey suggests that the first area that most men look at when they see a woman pass by is her face and chest. With that much emphasis on appearance, we become easily confused over love. We feel a sexual rush and wonder if love is paying a call.

Attraction to looks can be valuable, but it is definitely restricted to the realm of "like." Love cannot be based on what we see. This might seem obvious, but many couples have married because they liked each other's physical attributes. Others have rejected a magnificent person on the basis of size or muscle tone.

The Bible tells that God does not judge by outward appearance (Gal 2:6). That is our good example.

2. Personality

We enjoy being around pleasant people. If they are friendly and show interest in us, we like them. The person might be a good storyteller, clever, good conversationalist, well traveled, widely read, or whatever flips your switch. Possibly, he doesn't talk much, and that's right up your alley.

"Like" certainly applies to personality. We feel good being around the person. When he walks into the room, we perk up immediately because we are glad to see him.

Soon we believe that we would like to have him near us all the time. The person could tell jokes; you might laugh together at the overcooked roast; you would share the events of the day.

Personality stands at the border between love and like. This is a close call. He might be fun to be around, but is that reason enough to give him your heart?

3. Character

The arrow on the barometer glides past appearance and personality to enter the high love area. To "like" her is surface. To "love" her is a core issue. What is she really like? We discover this only by checking character. Have we looked at the value system, and do we love what we see?

By character we mean the person's

loyalty	sincerity
honesty	openness
dedication	caring
trustworthiness	morality
kindness	faith
patience	dependability

Many qualities can be added to the list. When appearance and personality begin to run thin, character is the lasting fiber which will hold love together.

When Boaz complimented Ruth he told her, "And now my daughter, don't be afraid. I will do for you all you ask. All my fellow townsmen know that you are a woman of noble character" (Ruth 3:11).

The book of Proverbs prizes character in marriage.

"A wife of noble character is a husband's crown " (Prov 12:4).

"Noble" shouldn't carry the idea of stuffy and aloof. Rather, the phrase means she has special strength. The Bible says that such a woman can be hard to find, but she is well worth the search (Prov 31:10).

Appearance and personality are both excellent attributes. The problem is that they aren't enough on which to hang a lasting love. Like nails driven into rotting wood, when we need to put any weight on them they will tear out of the wall.

Not the Marrying Kind

There are some excellent people who have no business getting married. Everyone likes them. They belong at backyard barbecues and are tons of fun on a retreat. Great surface people.

The problem is that they don't like to be tied down. If they can't get home at night, they don't want to have to call and check in. They are lousy at working things out with someone else. If you need them in a crisis, they might not show up.

Good people. Salt of the earth types. Just don't start loving them. Character is the only way to go.

31
False
Love

If someone goes duck hunting and knows nothing about the sport, he could end up shooting at anything. Each time a bird, a flock or a gaggle flies near, the bewildered amateur blasts off a few shots, hoping he might hit some feathered creature that looks like a duck.

Love is such a strong desire, and we are often so anxious about bagging this creature that the hunt becomes confusing. Unfamiliar with love and how to pursue it, we are apt to return home with the wrong "game" completely.

"I knew Bruce needed someone," Robin remembered. "His life was disheveled. He could barely cook; his apartment was a mess. I wanted to take care of him. If I took care of him, I was sure he would love me in return."

Boom. Robin shot both barrels, bagged Bruce and called it love. Unfortunately, when she got home and took a closer look, she saw that it wasn't love at all. From a distance, though, it had a few similar markings. For fifteen years they lived together with false love, not realizing what they had missed.

A catbird is one of nature's best imitators. It can sound like a bobolink or a kingfisher. A catbird can even make a noise like a croaking frog. You might have at some time been lured into your backyard because you thought you heard what sounded like a lost cat hiding in the trees. As you drew closer, you were surprised to see a mischievous catbird fly away.

There are also impostors posing as love. If we chase them, we could discover that we have been fooled by our own eagerness to find love.

Let's look at a few of the more frequent imitations which masquerade as love.

Pity Is False Love

Feeling sorry for yourself or for someone else can make you think you are in love.

John had a poor childhood; his mother didn't care for him; he had a slight learning disability. You think you can bundle him up and make his life new.

If love isn't the primary moving force, the two may regret the day they met. Join the Salvation Army, open a soup kitchen, collect clothing for the poor. One of the worst things anyone can do for John is to marry him out of pity and call it love. Over the years pity can turn into resentment and even hatred.

Self-pity is also false love. When someone wants to get married because he is afraid of being alone, he fools himself. The fear of loneliness is a lousy substitute for love.

Acceptance Is False Love

Afraid we will miss out on companionship or marriage is not the same as love. The frenzied search for a person to make our life complete clouds our concept of love.

The needs for security, acceptance, identity and friendship all look like love, but they will each fail to measure up. If you are desperate for acceptance, join the Jaycees or work with the Girl Scouts.

Sex Is False Love

If the truth were known, many couples are driven into each other's arms by racing hormones. (See chapter 15, "The Big Difference between Sex and Love.") Sex and love can be closely related, but they are not identical.

Most mornings we have to get out of bed and continue with our lives. Love will persevere when our bodies are tired, sick, injured and even dying. Sex is limited to its ability to thrill, entice and satisfy.

Sex is fantastic but it isn't love.

Escapism Is False Love

Rachel was swamped with problems. Her job was dead-end and boring. Every morning her car coughed and sputtered. Her parents were pushing Rachel to get an apartment of her own.

The only bright light in her foggy life was a young man named Derrick. Rachel thought maybe she loved Derrick, but she wasn't quite swept off her feet. Still, she wondered if her warm feelings for him might be close enough.

If she worked a bit harder at loving Derrick, she asked herself, couldn't she love him? Marrying Derrick could solve a lot of her problems and might lead to an easier life.

Rachel pushed love and escapism toward each other. Soon she couldn't tell apples from watermelons.

Rebounding Is False Love

We joke about loving someone on the rebound, but it's no laughing matter. If we split with someone and are unhappy with the separation, we might soon hurry to find another person to fill the empty spot.

Reeling from the experience, we ask questions like

Am I so terrible?

Will anyone else love me?

Why was I rejected?

Befuddled, we would welcome any vote of confidence. We want to be told that we are worth something. When a person glides up to our side, we might be thrilled at the attention.

How easily we could confuse that attention with love. How quickly we might love that attention. Attention and love mesh together and we are carried away.

Divorced persons can fall prey to false love, especially during the first few months. Couples who break up can become like magnets that are too eager to stick to another surface.

Martyrdom Is False Love

Dee has always wanted to work for Christ among the Indians of South America. She has met Ricky, who shares the same goals. Together, they talk of the "mission" that they could accomplish.

The world, the task, the service, the need become the center of their relationship. They speak of their love for Christ, their love for the Indians, but do they love each other?

Many famous couples appear to have loved their tasks more than they loved their partners. Goal-centered love is not personal love. Loving a cause and joining ranks to pursue that service is a dangerous relationship.

Parenthood Is False Love

The compulsive drive to have children is still strong and frequently muddles our thinking. A few of the more popular reasons for having children are

to establish equality with one's mother

to satisfy one's biological clock

to stay home from work

to create a life of one's own

These may have nothing to do with couple love. The person is looking for another person and has a hidden agenda: the strong desire to have children.

These are destructive reasons to conceive a child. That drive may become so powerful that love gets lost in the shuffle.

When children arrive and love doesn't, the result is one miserable couple. In the right context, at the right time, children are a great way to go.

Status Is False Love

The desire to be "Mrs. So and So"

The primary goal of having a magnificent wedding

The longing to marry a professional person

The concern to be with a "popular" person

The attraction to a person of power

The need to find someone with money

These are only samples of how we look for status. Our love for power or popularity gets mixed up with our love for the individual. Smart people step back and ask if they love the person or something about the person.

Status is a slick magician. It can fool the most alert of young lovers.

The pride of our heart can easily deceive us (Jer 49:16). We set our minds on a goal and tell ourselves it is love. The result can be terribly painful.

Look for real love, and the two of you can set goals together.

32
Two
Become
One

A movie star explained why she divorced her husband after eighteen months of marriage.

"Before I married Tony he had loads of girlfriends. Anywhere he went women literally threw themselves at him. Then we got married and naturally I assumed that part of his life would end. Apparently I assumed too much.

"Anytime Tony was away from home he slept with anyone he wanted. Faithfulness simply never occurred to him."

Couple love has a unique quality among humans. Two people say in effect, "I love you as I love no one else."

To love three women is a contradiction of couple love. Four people or three couplets do not a couple make. Two people in love is like no other form of human love.

Plural Love

We can love our neighbors. There is Dane down the street, Cheryl across the road and Dawn in the next apartment. We can love them each and all. We carry out their trash if they need help. While they are on vacation, we collect their newspapers and feed their dogs even if we can't stand mutts.

Each of us can love a dozen neighbors.

As parents we love our children. It would be unreasonable to love only one child out of the brood. Not only can we love each of them equally, but we are expected to. Anyone who tells us we should love Darren and not Timothy is a borderline ogre.

Parents have enough love to pour on a crateload of children.

The same is true if we have two living parents. We have the capacity to love both a mother and a father. It is unreasonable for a mother to say we can't also love her if we love our father. Even estranged parents must understand a child's capacity to love both parents.

Human love is like jelly and can be spread over many surfaces without depriving any area. But couple love doesn't have that pliability.

Couple Love

The ultimate goal of couple love is that two people will become one . . . not that three people will become a trio . . . or six people will create a committee. Couple love has a unique and narrow role.

Jesus Christ reminded us of the eternal principle. "The two will become one flesh" (Mt 19:5). The object of couple love is the merging of two people. In the merger they become one flesh but still manage to preserve their individual identities.

Some people protest. They want to pay allegiance to couple love but be romantically involved with others at the same time. They refuse to comprehend couple love. They want a boyfriend or girlfriend on the side.

They give lame excuses like

"I have too much love for one person."

"Lots of rich and famous people have more than one lover."

"I have physical needs."

"What's the big deal? Sex is just an activity."

These people show no respect or reverence for couple love. They want to talk about "running around" and you want to talk about merger, two different subjects.

Couple love does not have the elasticity of general love. Any attempt to stretch this love to cover others will only cause couple love to break.

One sock won't cover two feet. One romantic, merger-type love cannot include more than two people—one couple.

Anyone who doesn't appreciate union and faithfulness isn't ready for the adventure of couple love. They are still in search of group love, scattered love, sensual love, occasional love or some other derivative. But they are missing the genuine article.

Don't pretend that someone talking about coconuts is discussing peaches. If the person you love isn't interested in couple love, don't ignore that fact and act like they agree with you. A coconut is a coconut.

The author of Proverbs gives this guidance: "Let love and faithfulness never leave you; bind them around your neck, write them on the tablet of your heart" (3:3).

Couple love does not have a broad definition. It is the union, fusion, merger of two people. Only those who understand this are ready for it.

33
The Failure of Short-Love

If love is so much trouble, wouldn't we be better off with- out it? Much of what we read centers on the problems caused by love. There is so little said about its benefits. In some circles a great distrust has grown up as if to suggest that love is a massive pain but, like surgery, it must be done.

For a long time sex was extremely popular, but love was put down as naive or prudish. The battle cry seemed to be "Find someone, have a fast furious fling, and move on to another fling."

People believed in love in small doses . . . a few weeks, maybe several months if the person was special, then pick up your books, and personal belongings and move on. Love had become like a convenience store: a good place to rush in and then drive off quickly.

Love was seen as confining, strangling, limiting. The very word sounded claustrophobic. Like cranberry juice, half a small glass would be pleasant, but who would want an entire bottleful?—or so the argument went.

As a practical matter, short-love fails to satisfy. Short-love is intensified and exciting but by its quick nature leaves each partner frustrated. Like anxiety, short-love can never rest, because the people involved must go back to the hunt every few days or weeks or months. The hunt takes pauses, but it is never over.

If someone tinkers with short-love, many deficiencies quickly become apparent. Those failings explain why so many have given it up to look for a more permanent relationship.

Short-Love Is Lonely
Part of the reason we love is to find a person who cares for us and who will become our companion. That's one key reason God gave us marriage.

Short-love sends a glaring message which says: "This relationship is temporary. There's nothing dependable or permanent about it. Before too long you will be back out in the emotional cold looking for another companion."

The odds of couple love which leads to marriage lasting for fifty years might not be as high as we would like, but the odds of short-love lasting are small at best. Short-love will almost certainly fail our needs for dependability.

Entering new relationships is extremely painful for most of us. That's why we are often afraid to date, afraid to make the phone call, afraid to take risks and let people know exactly who we are. Short-love guarantees continuous agony.

"I hate starting all over again. The uncertainty and stress of trying to get to know another person. But loneliness is a terror. I have to keep finding a relationship," Teri explained.

Like salmon swimming upstream, it's something we are driven to do, but it's no fun trip.

Short-Love Is Antichild

Eventually our thoughts turn to having children. There are a few people who want to raise them alone, but most of us see the need for a couple, if at all possible.

We want the best for our child, and a full complement of steady parents matches that dream. Switching from partner to partner, searching for love in motels, entertaining "houseguests" for two months at a time . . . to most of us doesn't sound like wholesome child care.

The pressure will build. The clock is ticking. The words *children* and *family* have a nice rhythm. *Single parent* speaks more of harsh reality than of cozy household.

Even if we have raced head-on to establish a career, many will stop to wonder if something tremendously important is bypassing them. Children can be one of the deepest pleasures in life. A series of intermittent, meteor-type relationships offer scarce hope of producing that promise.

Stacey is a sad example of a series of mini-loves gone sour. She has two children, each fathered by a different man. Neither male was worth marrying, in Stacey's estimation, and she isn't sure they would have married anyway. As best as she is able, the twenty-two year old is trying to instigate a relationship with a third man.

Stacey insists that mini-loves suit her temperament. Understandably, Stacey is also beginning to see how they work against her goal of raising children in a loving atmosphere.

Short-Love Is Dangerous

People who are committed to long-range, permanent love do not suffer from sexually transmitted diseases. This is a phenomenon almost exclusively reserved for short-love.

Anyone standing around in a bar or lounge looking for quickie love is a prime candidate. Millions of singles protest that this isn't true, but millions of others know better. Chastity has become more popular in some circles because young adults are facing the facts.

Married people frequently stray, and they become at risk. They have taken a bit of time out of their commitment and are searching for mini-love. For a few hours or a weekend they break their vows and put their marriage partner at risk for the pleasure of a quick encounter.

But married people who stay home are almost never in harm's way. This is what the Bible euphemistically calls drinking out of our own well (Prov 5:15). The same passage then warns us: "Let them be yours alone, never to be shared with strangers" (5:17).

Short-Love Is Emotionally Painful

Many lovers tinkering with our hearts are apt to leave them in disrepair. Numerous loves are likely to strain this part, damage that spring or overload another section. Frequently, disillusionments harden a heart and leave it reluctant to trust, believe and enjoy.

The singles scene gets into full swing for a few years, and then the tragedies begin to peak. Eventually, their numbers and severity are overwhelming. Frustrated and worn out, they back off and long for lasting love instead of the instant-capsule variety.

Emotions are tied to a rope. We are afraid to cut them loose, because we know our feelings will get hurt. Tethered emotions make for restrained and strained relationships.

Short-love says, "I will give you part of my heart for a little while, I think."

Short-Love Is Fragile

"I've been thinking about going to my parents' place for Christmas, and I was wondering if you'd be interested in going along."

He replies, "That could be fun. Let's see what the winter brings."

After all, who knows what tomorrow will bring. But he is saying more than that. As a short-termer, he doesn't know if he will be around three months from now.

A note on the kitchen table, a phone call one evening, an argument over who paid for supper and this relationship is in the morgue. How does it affect a couple to know that they are always about two heated discussions from one or the other of them packing their duffle bags?

Every relationship is tentative, but short-love is fragile. By their very nature, neither person is permitted to relax and enjoy the other. The important ingredient of security is missing. Most relationships should find a balance between freedom and security. Short-love offers carloads of freedom and spoonfuls of security. There is practically no safety and only a murky future. Normally, love should produce a sense of protection. Love should offer more safety than high walls or fortified defenses.

"Love and faithfulness keep a king safe; through love his throne is made secure" (Prov 20:28).

Short-love makes walls of sand. It takes no outrageous flood to tear it down. Regular tides or a few irregular waves and everything might be gone.

Chart the conversation of a couple who are not committed to the long run. Listen for tentative words and phrases like "if," "maybe," "we'll see," "that's a long way off," "let's take it one day at a time." Is there a fragileness which makes even the immediate future uncertain? Short-love wants to be free to give all its energy to love. Instead, its attention is drawn from the love and concentrates on the shortness. Their relationship is not defined by love but rather by brevity, the overriding element.

Committed love has its problems. Half the population has critical difficulties with committed, extended love. Despite that, the inadequacies of short-love are staggering. Short-love is so impotent it barely qualifies as love at all.

34

Becoming More Lovable

*T*hat's just the way I am. I can't help it. If people don't like me this way, there isn't anything I can do about it."

There is some truth to that statement. Fortunately, it isn't all true. We can make a conscious effort to improve our lovability. Personality transplants are rare, but personality enhancement is a real possibility.

Without becoming too introspective, go over the following list and ask if there is one way you could improve yourself under each point. Most of us have these basic qualities, but we often allow them to droop. For instance, we are capable of being patient, but too often we let our patience slide and impatience becomes an overriding characteristic. We can safely say that impatience fails to make us more lovable. Irritability is prickly. It's no love potion. Rudeness isn't a charmer.

What are the chief traits that make a person more lovable? Reflect for a moment, and ask how you can improve yourself and become more lovable.

A Dozen Ways to Become More Lovable

1. Become more considerate.

Love is not self-centered. Look for ways to make the other person's life run more smoothly. Help carry packages, volunteer to run errands, wash his car, say "please" and "thank you," drop things off at the post office.

"But I already do that," we object. Great. Now find two more things and do those too. We tend to love people who act lovingly.

Don't wait to be asked. Think ahead of what someone else is facing, and anticipate her needs. Consideration takes a right balance. Be careful not to take over, but try to make life a bit easier for others.

2. Check your appearance.

Looks aren't everything, but neither are they unimportant. It is all right to work in a pigpen, but it is inexcusable to look like one.

Key in on cleanliness. Even the most pleasant person is hard to love if he flunks soap.

Appearance is the gate through which most of us must go. Reasonable care will make that opening more likely to happen. Sensible maintenance can help make the relationship last longer.

3. Aim for even-temperedness.

It's hard to hug a geyser, especially an irregular one. Will it blow up any minute? Will the hole be dry one day and shooting for the sky the next?

Severe mood swings leave other people off balance and apprehensive. We become leery of the person rather than drawn to him.

Maybe your mood expressions are too extreme. Try to avoid getting up too high or down too low. Rolling hills are easier to enjoy than are enormous mountains and plummeting valleys.

4. Share yourself.

We love what we know, and we fear what we don't know. Disclosure is the key to giving others the real you. Vulnerability makes the real you available to love.

This isn't easy for most of us; however, as we pull back each layer of resistance, we show more of us to love. We are afraid that disclosure means someone will see how ugly we are. In fact just the opposite is likely to happen.

Sharing yourself understandably seems risky. Do it in short shots if necessary. Let your emotions surface and show your genuine self. This could take a great deal of practice for some of us.

5. Become patient and understanding.

These are two of the most basic Christian attributes. The Spirit of God helps us distribute these in generous proportions.

It's difficult to love an intolerant person. How can I get close to you if I know you might bite my head off at any moment? How can I disclose myself to you if I think you could never understand?

Love is seriously shackled if a person is rigid and unsympathetic. When we try to put ourselves in the shoes of others, we increase our lovability.

6. Become a great listener.

We like a good storyteller, but we love a good story listener. If you want to be admired, encourage someone to tell you more about what interests him. Listening is an art which takes practice. Ask three questions:

How much do we listen to others?

How much do we encourage others to talk?

How much do we talk?

Balance is the goal. We can change our ratio of talk and listen.

7. Be affectionate.

Cardboard people are tough to love. It happens. All of us know some stiff, standoffish person whom we simply adore. But that person makes love more work than it should be.

Concentrate on touching. Give shoulder rubs and hugs, touch hands. Occasionally, get into your friend's space.

If you exchange something—money, a package, a book—make it a habit to touch your friend's finger, hands or arms (without mauling or assuming some reptilian hold on the person). Few experiences are as loving as making nonthreatening contact with a caring person.

Affectionate behavior might not come easily—it doesn't for millions of us—but practice will increase your ability to handle it.

Most discussions of love for young adults suggest that they become less affectionate. We ought to remind ourselves that the fear of touching can become too great. Middle ground is the most comfortable.

8. Try optimism.

Do you have a friend who sees the bleak side of everything? He complains because gold is heavy. He throws stones at robins because he doesn't like singing.

The grouch is still on your friend list, but you have to admit the person causes you grief. We are drawn more readily to someone who is cheery and has a hopeful outlook, the old "We can get it done" attitude.

"I feel discouraged every time I'm around her." When people say that, they will begin to spend less time with her.

Make upbeat, hopeful, encouraging, progressive statements.

9. Speak with confidence.

Whining is no aphrodisiac. Do we regularly recite a litany of things we can't do?

I'm not much of an athlete.

It's not one of those thinking games, is it?

I've never been much at making decisions.

I hate trying new things.

Check your tone. Do your conversations drone on and do your words put you down?

Try phrases like

"I think I can."

"I enjoy new things."

"Let's see how it works."

"I want to improve."

"I'm putting my future together."

Maybe we aren't aware of the bent our statements are taking.

10. Practice generosity.

Volunteer to drive; offer to pay when it's reasonable; take the hard job. Some of us sit back and appear to take advantage of every situation. We act like life is a game, and we are out to get the most that we can with the least amount of effort. It's harder to love someone who is basically a taker. We are drawn more to givers.

11. Work on being sociable.

Invite people over to visit you, and become comfortable in social settings. Wallflowers are frequently people who design their lifestyle to include as few contacts as possible. Consequently, they look dreary, act isolated and then complain because no one digs them out of their cave.

Sociability is an effort, and we usually decide whether or not we'll be sociable. As one girl said, "It occurred to me that if I chose to lock myself in my room and remain there, no one else would really care."

Life isn't usually quite that dismal for most of us, but it's close. We can never count on someone else to break down the social barriers we work so diligently to erect.

12. Be supportive.

Is someone facing a problem? Loan out your books on the subject. Is someone going downtown? Offer a ride—offer your car if necessary. Is a friend going on a trip? Insist on collecting the mail and taking care of the pooch.

Don't demand that your help be accepted. Pushy people can be obnoxious. Just offer your help in a way that is sincere, letting the person know that you can be counted on.

When we find the correct attitude of wanting to help but not to dominate—wanting to help but without taking over—we can become extremely attractive people.

In the process of creating Adam and Eve God noticed that Adam still needed a "suitable helper" (Gen 2:20). We all do. Whether male or female, suitable helpers will always be wanted, appreciated and loved.

If we feel shallow in love, we can grow. First, we need to work at becoming more loving. As we become more loving, we also become increasingly lovable.

Paul was excited to see this in the lives of the Philippian Christians. "And this is my prayer: that your love may abound more and more in knowledge and depth of insight" (Phil 1:9).

Love does not have to be stagnant. Neither does lovability. We can work at becoming more lovable.

35
Love Is Well Worth It!

*L*ove is for everybody. Whether we marry and have a nursery full of children or remain single and work at a mall, we enjoy the experience of loving and being loved. Life without any form of love would be bleak.

When we see the opportunity to love, we should go for it. Break out of your plastic bubble, and reach for the hand of another person. Loving trees, books or sports will never compare with the enormous joy of loving a person and being loved in return.

Whether we love a parent, a friend, a class full of children or a partner, love is an emotion too fulfilling for anyone to miss.

How do we know the value of people except through love? How do we understand the fellowship of God unless we experience the longing for the company of another person? How do we begin to comprehend the sacrifice of Christ on a cross until we have worried about the safety of someone we care about?

To love is to make contact with life as God intended life to be. To be without love is to be lonely, isolated and brittle. Love provides the warmth and reassurance that make life worthwhile.

No wonder this old saying survives: "It is better to have loved and lost than never to have loved at all."

Even the pain which accompanies love is an agony worth knowing. The disappointments, the confusion, the soul-searching all have meaning because they are mixed into a feast like none other on earth.

God has placed inside us a buoyant hope. Even if we have seen parents or friends love and then lose, even if we have known the shattering setback of lost love, we eventually pop up on the surface and choose to love again.

Love calls each of us. As a good tune sets your foot tapping in reflex, love simply seems natural. As spring pulls us out-of-doors and almost demands that we enjoy the sunshine, love is a compelling force. God made it that way, and we would be foolish to turn our backs on his great gift.

Look for someone who turns your head, for someone who ransacks your mind, for a person who shortens your attention span. Look for a person who increases your heart rate and leaves you in a trance.

Look for that person, and love him with all of your heart. God has been good.